If You Were Arrested For Selling,

would there be enough evidence to convict you?

A Sales Effectiveness Handbook

Second Edition

written

Ian Selb

CEO & President

Power Marketing International Inc.

Dedicated to my family:

Leah, Nicole, Julie, Mitchell, Cindy

and

The incredible team of professionals at
Power Marketing

SECOND EDITION

Printed in Canada by Friesens

Cover designed by Clare Gray

Layout designed by Clare Gray

ISBN 1-55383-056-3

Table of Contents

CHAPTER ONE

Introduction to the author and his journey

Ian Selbie

Founder, CEO and President

Power Marketing International Inc.

Are sales people born or built? Is selling an art form or a science? These two questions are very interesting and have been debated through time. I believe sales people are built and the process of selling is a science. When we think of great sales people, what skills or characteristics make them great? Integrity? Communication skills? Organization? Persistence?

Confidence? A caring Attitude? These may come to mind, but were these people born with these abilities or did they develop them over time? Was Tiger Woods born a great golfer? Was Wayne Gretzky born a great hockey player? Was Mark McGuire born a great home run hitter? These professionals may have had some innate abilities, but they all developed their skills and abilities through learning, dedication, practice and determination. I believe this is how great sales people are developed.

I started my selling career in 1979 with Olivetti Canada, an Italian based typewriter and word processing company. I had a sales territory in Richmond, British Columbia, selling typewriters door to door. The next step in my journey was as an entrepreneur, selling personal computers in the early 80's with Kaypro and Eagle PC's running the CP/M operating system with word processing, spreadsheets and accounting software. In 1984 I joined Apple Canada, the Canadian subsidiary of Apple Computer, who that year had announced the Macintosh personal computer. My first sales role with Apple was developing and managing Apple resellers and channel partners in British Columbia. Apple had an incredible culture. I still remember attending my first international sales conference in Hawaii. The theme of the conference was "Blue Busters", a spin on the then popular song "Ghost Busters" from the hit movie. The Blue in Blue Busters, of course meant big blue, IBM. Steve Jobs, co-founder and then CEO stepped up on stage and addressed the Apple sales force. He described his vision so dramatically and visually that he ignited the entire room with passion. It was like an address from General Patton.

However, the analogy of David and Goliath would have been more appropriate. Like David, we believed in the vision and were confident in our pursuit of the industry Goliath, IBM.

Ian Selbie with Steve Jobs 1984

After 4 years in channel partner management I took on the challenge of corporate accounts for Apple. In 1989, I was a member of an incredible sales team. Our sales manager, and one of my mentors to this day, was Ian Adam, (xIBM, xOlivetti) In corporate accounts was Brad Duholke (xIBM) In channel accounts was Willie Palmarini (xOlivetti) also a life mentor. In education accounts was Andy Bridges (xDEC) and our favorite systems engineer was Alan Vintr, who understood business and technology. This was an incredible team. We challenged and brought out the best in each other, something I know Ian Adam is proud of to this day. In the early '90s my role expanded and included branch management during the downsizing years at Apple. My most memorable time at Apple was in 1990 at the

Worldwide Sales Conference, when I was recognized by Apple as their top sales person. I had two corporate accounts that our team had done a fabulous job with, BC Hydro and British Columbia Automobile Association.

In late 1993 I left Apple to launch the Vancouver branch of Sybase, a relational database company. After 9 months and losing 2 very large deals to Oracle, I realized that in these few short months I had learned more about selling than I had in 10 years at Apple. In our two day consultative sales training program I describe some tough sales lessons I learned as a result of my failure at Sybase. I stopped the bleeding at Sybase by taking a sales management position with SHL Systemhouse. It was then that I decided I needed to have my own business, something I could be passionate about, like the good years at Apple.

In the fall of 1994, I attended a business seminar in Vancouver entitled Success '95. There were a number of 'Top Billed' speakers present, such as Zig Ziglar, Jim Rohn and David Chilton, including Robert Schullar, a minister of the Crystal Cathedral Church in California. Schullar began his presentation by saying "I'm a pastor of a church, what do I know about business success? I know many successful business people and they all have a plan for success which comes down to four things." With this he had my attention, and I knew right then and there that I was going to start my own business. But of course along with that passion I had many concerns, although having only 4 things to focus on encouraged me to believe I could do it.

Let me share with you what Robert Schullar shared with us that fall day in 1994:

1) Start to play... find your passion, what you love doing, what you've already had success at doing. If life was free, what would you want to do? For me, I love selling, coaching people, and presenting. I get a high from watching sales people "get it." I love seeing their confidence grow.

2) Stop to pray... ask God to help you, put him on your team, make him CEO (in my case CEO and CFO) and remember to thank him for your success. I was already an early Christian at this time and felt strongly that I could accomplish this step.

3) Prepare to pay... if you are going to pursue your dreams, your passion, your love, there will need to be some sacrifices of your time, your effort and your income. All of these areas will be impacted. Looking back on our first five years of business at Power Marketing, I worked harder, put in more time and effort than at any other job I've had. I feel blessed by my faith and labors because my income was not negatively impacted.

1) Start to Play
2) Stop to Pray
3) Prepare to Pay
4) Plan to Stay

4) Plan to stay... In everything you do, do it with the long term in mind. Build relationships of integrity and honesty with customers, employees, suppliers, alliances and investors. I understood the importance of relationships and how critical a good network was. Looking back, my early clients and employees came from my network. I can not understate the importance of this. I remember my father Sandy Selbie telling me years ago, "Ian, it's not just what you know, it's also who you know".

A week after attending this seminar I began writing my business plan and first sales training program, which in early 1995 became Power Marketing Communications. This would allow me to sell, present, teach and coach people on a topic I loved, sales and sales management. It wasn't long after I wrote my business plan, that I resigned from SHL to launch Power Marketing in Vancouver.

Today Power Marketing International Inc. is a well regarded leader of sales management consulting, training, coaching and software services. We have helped companies around the world achieve their revenue and margin objectives through a proven set of sales and marketing services. Our clients operate in a number of market segments, from high technology and advertising to financial services and manufacturing.

Achieving sales effectiveness is a journey, and our services have been designed to help our clients get there. The sales and marketing services we use to help our clients become effective selling organizations include; Annual Sales and Markting audit, Sales and Marketing Assessments, Consultative Sales Training & Management Training, On-going Sales Management Coaching and Sales Management Software.
My wife Cindy and I, along with our 4 children, Leah, Nicole, Julie and Mitchell, live in White Rock, BC, a small southern

suburb of Vancouver. I tell Cindy that if our life was already paid for, that from a career perspective there is nothing I'd rather do than what Power Marketing enables me to do: help sales people and sales managers reach their potential, for me this has been so rewarding.

In our experience with our client's, senior management, sales management and sales people, regardless of industry, we find sales organizations repeatedly making the same classic mistakes. We author a series of executive white papers, one being "The Seven Deadly Sins in Selling." The objective of the white paper and these next few pages is to provide you with an opportunity to compare the behavior of your sales force with our findings. How many of the deadly sins are your sales force committing?

THE SEVEN DEADLY SINS IN SELLING

Sin #1 - Calling at non-decision making levels

In the highly dynamic world of selling, there are two very desirable words: "Yes," and a quick "No." The slow "No" robs sales people of their most precious asset, their time. The quick "No" allows sales people to move on to opportunities they can win. The most significant contributor to the "slow No" is calling at non-decision making levels. Spending time talking to middle managers and influencers of prospective clients not only creates a slow "No," it commits your level of contact in the account. Once established at the influencer level you are now at their mercy in terms of moving up to meet with the executive level, where the real decisions are made. In fact, to get the meeting with the executive, you may need to climb over the influencer, putting your relationship and chances for success at risk. Always calling high first, can more than double your company's win percentage.

Question: On new business opportunities, what would increasing your win ratio by 100% do for your total revenue?

Sin#2 - Believing it's a "closing problem" when it's always a "qualifying problem"

When we meet company presidents for the first time we often hear, "Our sales people are keen, enthusiastic, high energy people, but they struggle with closing. Can you help us?" After we complete our assessment and facilitate our sales training program, it becomes clear that it is never a closing problem, but failure to diligently qualify opportunities that cause the loss of the deal. There are 7 key elements to qualifying a deal. One of the most overlooked is failing to understand the prospective client's business pain, not just what they need, but why they need it. So think of it as the cause, not the effect. Most sales people who are focused on trying to "close the deal" find the harder they push, the further away the deal gets. Twenty percent of the sales people in the world are making eighty percent of the commissions. The other 80% are fighting over the crumbs. These top guns are where they are, not because of closing skills, but because they know how to qualify their opportunities and invest their time appropriately.

Questions: What percentage of new opportunities pursued last year did your sales force lose? How many of these should have been abandoned earlier in the process because they didn't qualify? How many would you have won if your sales force was diligently qualifying?

Sin #3 - Failure to follow a systematic, consistent sales process, team wide.

When conducting sales and marketing assessments for clients, we find as many sales processes in a company as there are sales people. The absence of a systematic approach creates three significant challenges for sales organizations. The first challenge is a lack of consistency with customers. Each sales person uses his own approach which differs from customer to customer, it also creates a sales management nightmare. We define good sales management as a proactive coach and mentor of the sales force. To be an effective coach, sales managers must be an expert in the process themselves, but how can a sales manager be an expert in ten or more processes? Finally, perhaps the most painful issue is inaccurate revenue forecasting.

Questions: How many sales people do you have? How many sales processes do they have? How accurate are your sales force's revenue forecasts? What are the costs to your business due to inaccurate revenue forecasting?

Sin #4 - The premature proposal trap

What is the fastest way to get rid of a sales person? Ask for a proposal? The sales person usually hurries back to his office to begin his proposal building process, and for some sales people this is a major work of art. After countless hours, perhaps days of work the sales person calls the prospective client and says "when can I show you our proposal?" The unqualified prospect replies "Oh, just fax it over, we're real busy over here, but I'll read it this week" A week passes and the sales person follows up only to learn that the prospect has not read it, but has told the sales person to follow up in 6 months. Sound familiar? Add insult to injury with the fact that the sales person was probably forecasting the deal. Never create a proposal for a prospective client without a diligent client needs assessment and qualification process. If the prospect is not willing to invest time in having you better understand his needs, then he's probably not really interested. Equally important, yet so often overlooked, is to always present your proposal in person to the entire decision making team. Some sales people trust their contact within the client's organization to present their proposal for them. The problem with this is that the contact is not qualified to represent your company's value; they are not a sales person. They can't speak from experience about the many other satisfied reference customers your company has. They cannot thoroughly explain any details about your proposal that may need discussion.

Questions: How many proposals does your company produce in a year? How many of these proposals were created without first conducting a thorough client needs assessment and qualifying the opportunity? How many proposals did your sales force present in person last year? Through proper qualification, and presenting your proposals in person you can increase your win percentage by at least 25%. What would this mean to your company?

Sin #5 - Not having a documented sales plan with measurable goals and objectives

The phrase, "If you fail to plan, you plan to fail," is especially true in sales. Beyond having an annual sales quota, every sales person needs to have a plan to achieve, or in fact over achieve their numbers. Sales people need to build an annual strategy, broken down into monthly goals and objectives. The sales person and sales manager should review these goals quarterly and make any needed adjustments to ensure the completion of the plan. This sin is as much an issue for sales people as it is for sales managers. Sales people need a personal sales plan for success every year. Strategy, activity and then results, is the "ready, aim, fire" of a good sales plan.

Question: How confident are you in your existing documented sales plan? How many times during the year do your sales managers and sales people formally sit down to review the progress made on their personal sales plans?

Sin #6 - Failure to utilize the most effective sales weapon you have - your existing customers

Many sales organizations use notebook computers today, but in most cases, after the high tech honeymoon wears off, they come to the realization that for the most part, sales people don't sell anything while in front of a computer screen. Yes there are smart electronic applications that help sales people plan, learn, prepare and present. We use email with clients and colleagues, gather client information from web sites before our sales call, use contact databases and schedulers, forecasting tools and of course, presentation and proposal tools. However they all take a back seat to the most powerful sales tool a sales person has: the power of proof, or the reference customer. We work with a wide range of companies and usually discover they are not fully leveraging their existing customers to help them succeed. In our two day sales training program, which is always followed up by our sales management coaching program, we teach the 7 "R's" of consultative selling. The principles behind four of them are as follows:

- Relationship... Develop a trusted advisor relationship with your client.
- Reference... As a part of your account management process, ask for a written letter of reference.
- Repeat... By virtue of the added value your client receives from you, you'll earn repeat business.
- Referral... A satisfied client will provide you with referrals to new opportunities.

Questions: How many current letters of reference from existing customers do you have? How many customers do you have? If a customer does not want to give you a letter, learn why not, then address it.

Sin #7 – Thinking that sales software CRM will cure an inconsistent or ineffective sales process.

Good process must precede tools and this is clearly true in the world of sales. To illustrate this I want to use the game of golf as a working example. Do you play golf? Or as I refer to it, chasing a little white ball around for 5 hours! Do you know what I mean when I say I have a slice? Oh You too! A very common issue for the amateur golfer. Well as it turns out the golf swing is a process - a series of actions that need to happen in the proper sequence in order for the right outcome to occur. This is exactly what a golf swing is. Now for us slicers, what do you think happens if we run back to the pro shop and buy one of those oversized, huge drivers? Now what happens to our slice? You may have actually done this, I certainly have, you actually get better at slicing, or, go deeper into the trees, making your game worse, not better. This can be a lot like sales software or CRM systems. Hoping to fix your ineffective or inconsistent sales process, you decide to purchase the big driver - yes, the great big new software. A few weeks go by and your sales people do not see the value in using it. We've heard sales people say things like "it takes longer to put the information into the system than it did to meet the customer…" or "I get absolutely nothing in return for my time in using the system…"

It turns out that step one in implementing sales software or CRM has nothing to do with software, it's all about process. The right sales process, supported by a sales management methodology and you're ready for the power tools. As in the game of golf, it's our swing that needs work, along with lessons and perhaps, a little practice?

Question: How confident are you in your existing documented sales plan? How many times during the year do your sales managers and sales people formally sit down to review the progress made on their personal sales plan?

Summary

True sales effectiveness is not just a campaign or company slogan of the month. It is an attitude and commitment to continual listening, learning, refinement and development. This commitment must start at the top with senior management. Only then can this journey begin. We hope these few pages on the 7 sins has been useful in helping you evaluate your company's sales effectiveness. Should you decide that your sales organization needs improvement, we would be pleased to help you. Our web site address is www.powermarketingworld.com.

CHAPTER TWO

The Model of Sales Effectiveness

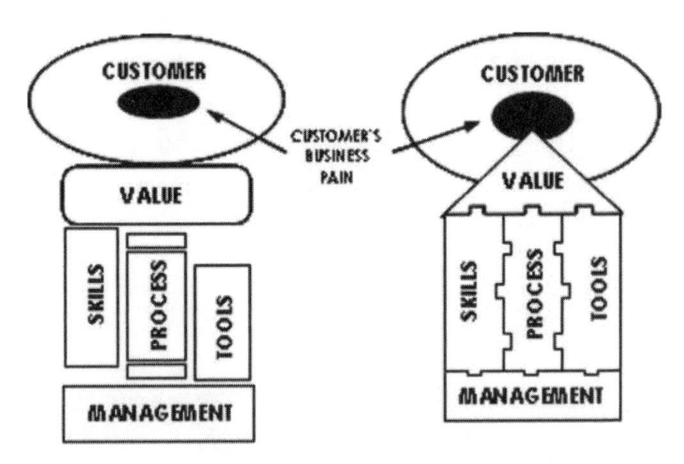

The Typical Sales Organization

The Model of Sales Effectiveness

The illustration depicts two distinctly different sales approaches. While true sales effectiveness is a challenge, we believe it is definitely possible. There are six elements to true sales effectiveness:

1) Value Proposition
2) Sales Process
3) Sales Skills
4) Sales Tools
5) Sales Management
6) The Customer

The model on the left of the previous page is typical of most sales organizations. We refer to this as the "old model of push-based selling," which is ineffective in today's highly competitive business world. The model on the right represents true sales effectiveness - all of the elements work together and are targeted at the customer's business pain.

VALUE PROPOSITION

What is a value proposition? We define it as "the value of your company's products and services articulated in your customer's terminology, complete with quantifiable business justification". Said simply, "the reason your customers do business with you." Often as companies grow and change, a gap between leadership and field sales develops. The original value the company presented to its clients becomes watered down or even forgotten. There are two other major factors that contribute to the erosion of a value proposition. First, pressure from competitors, neutralizing or commoditizing your value proposition and secondly, the changing needs of the customer. Who defines value? The sales person? The company the sales person works for? The industry? Only customers define value, so as a customer's business changes, grows, evolves, so do their needs and thus what value means to them. There is tangible merit in understanding your value proposition and then making it intrinsic in everything you do. Build it into your entire selling approach, your marketing materials, your message, your delivery, and equally important, your attitude. Understanding your customer and positioning your company's value proposition are the first steps towards sales effectiveness.

SALES PROCESS

We define the sales process starting with "proactive lead creation" all the way through to "leveraging reference customer." In our experience, most sales organizations have as many sales processes as sales people, which assumes that each sales person is consistent with every prospect. This lack of process consistency creates three challenges for companies.

"An effective and consistent sales process is a blueprint for success"

1. Communication consistency issues with customers and prospects.

2. Sales management nightmare, as a good sales manager need to be a proactive coach and mentor to the sales process. How can any sales manager be an expert of several processes?

3. Revenue forecasting accuracy. The largest cause of inaccurate revenue forecasting is an inconsistent sales process. Does qualified in New York, mean qualified in Toronto or LA? Most companies do not have a formalized sales

process and consequently cannot determine how to improve it. Understanding your sales process can answer a wealth of questions: "At which point in the process are we losing customers? Are we calling the right people? Are we presenting our value proposition to the right people at the right time? Do we have a system for listening and understanding our customers?" An effective sales process must be streamlined in order for the entire sales force to adopt it and make it their own.

SALES SKILLS DEVELOPMENT

In the area of sales skills, many sales organizations have some trained people, usually with no commonality in methods or process. In many cases, there is a lack of commitment towards an ongoing skills development process. Most professions, such as medicine, law, management consulting, sports, etc., require professionals to practice and fine-tune their game. This ongoing commitment is what makes them professional. Many companies say their people are their biggest asset or differentiator; however, not investing in these people is a common oversight. Highly effective sales organizations have an ongoing commitment to professional development of the entire sales team, not just the quota-carrying sales people. Failure to develop your sales peoples' skill levels can have a dramatic cost affect to your organization. "How many sales people do you have? How many sales calls do they make per week? Is every call a highly effective call?" Each ineffective call has a real cost to your company. A commitment from management to continually developing the skill levels of the sales force is a critical step towards sales effectiveness.

SALES TOOLS

Sales tools should be focused on assisting the customer driven company in its efforts to identify, educate, qualify, motivate and influence customers. The area of sales tools is very much in vogue today, with the lure of sales automation and its promise of sales productivity. In recent studies, over 70% of companies who invest in sales force automation fail to have their expectations met - most fail. The sales tools must be mapped to the sales process, not the process mapped to the tool. Most companies buy notebook computers and software and wait for new sales records to be set. Sales tools are not just limited to technology; videos, brochures, customer needs assessments, white papers and customer reference letters for example, can also be excellent tools in the hands of the sales force. It is critical that these tools be easy to use and not administration intensive. After all, they should help the sales force, not hinder them.

SALES MANAGEMENT

Most sales managers have been promoted through the sales ranks. Good sales people don't necessarily make good managers. In fact, selling and sales management do not have much in common. Parenting and sales management are more closely linked. Today's sales manager needs to coach, assist, train, motivate, and plan with their sales people while staying in touch with the needs of the customer. Most sales managers, as mentioned, have been promoted from sales, being told "here's your new corner office, business cards, giant sales quota, so make it happen!" Companies tend to overlook the fact that this new leader needs to develop coaching and leadership skills in order to be effective. Most sales managers have a lack of management currency, meaning the tools and processes to put themselves in a coaching and mentoring role. Sales managers need to be integrated into the areas of skills development, sales process and sales tools in order to contribute to sales effectiveness in their capacity as sales leader.

THE CUSTOMER

One of the most telling oversights a sales person can make is failure to thoroughly understand the needs of their customer. How can a doctor prescribe a remedy without knowing the problem, and what caused it? Most sales people at best, try to understand what the customer needs, without really understanding why they need it. The why is their business pain. Consultative selling requires the sales professional to be intimate with the problems, needs, objectives and business pains of their customers. The objective is to earn the rank as the customer's consultative advisor, not just another commission breathing, pushy sales person.

THE OVER-ENGINEERED COMPANY

Today's business environment is ripe for the consultative sales person to play a strategic role with their customers. Why? The 90's was the decade of corporate re-engineering, right sizing and down sizing. However most companies who survived these corporate evolutions have less people to do the same or more business. Many companies have been cut back across the entire organization, leaving fewer people to do much more than ever before. What companies used to "insource" or do themselves, they now look to "outsource" or seek outside help to accomplish.

Many of these companies tried to reengineer themselves, by finding new more efficient ways and processes to operate their business. Most companies "cut without changing," in fact many over-cut and lost customers as a result. I'm sure you can think of a few in this category. These companies in many cases have no "soul." The passion that fueled their initial growth has been impacted as a result of the re-engineering process. This is usually evidenced by the attitudes and morale of the people in the company. Business must go on, but many in these firms are saying to themselves, "How can I get it all done with so few resources?" This sounds like music to the consultative sales person's ear. Never before has there been such an opportunity for sales people to raise the bar and play a much more strategic role for their customers. Companies who once had teams of people to drive business initiatives now have a few, and the consultative sales person can be a highly effective trusted advisor/consultant to their customers.

COMPANY TYPES

People have character and style, and so do companies. We have categorized companies into four distinct groups:

- Change Company
- Growth Company
- Status Quo Company
- Pleased and Proud Company

The Change Company is one who is changing its business proactively or reactively. It may have been forced to change due to external factors in the market, competitors, economics, technology, globalization, margin pressures, etc. It is, or has been through a business re-engineering or right sizing process. Companies in this category do recognize their business pain and usually have the funding required to make the appropriate changes. They are an attractive prospect for a sales person because they have pain, and funding.

The Growth Company is on the up and up. Growing quickly, they need to build their infrastructure, and need resources to continue their growth. These are also attractive prospects for a sales person, because funding is usually not a problem and they have well defined needs. These companies will not spend months and months on requests for proposals because their needs are usually of an urgent nature. In fact they may pay more for quick delivery to address their urgent needs.

The Status Quo Company does not perceive that it has business pain. Perhaps an "itch," but not real "pain." It may acknowledge things could be better, but its moniker is "let's not fix what isn't really broken." It is cautious and avoids risk and its decisions can take a long time to make. It has no perceived pain or urgency, and has not assigned any funding. Not an attractive prospect for a sales person. However let's not forget them, because the business environment and people will change and they may end up in the "change company" category down the road. Even an ostrich pulls its head out of the sand eventually.

The Pleased and Proud Company believes that they have done a fabulous job solving their problems. In fact they may have considered marketing them selves because they are proud of their internal initiatives. These companies have no pain. In fact, they think they manufactured the "gain." Thus, they are not attractive as a prospect. Again they should not be forgotten, because their needs may change with time and turnover.

CHAPTER THREE

The Value Proposition

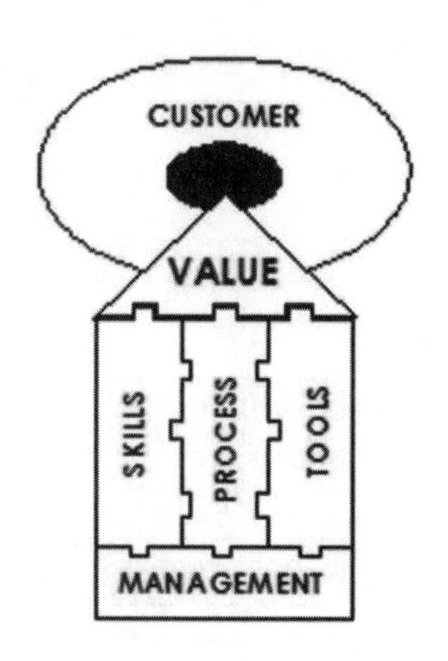

You find yourself on the twentieth floor of a downtown building in corporate North America. You get on the elevator, press lobby, look up and say "hello" to the individual in the elevator. They return your hello as the doors close, look you straight in the eye and say "What do you do?" You have 20 floors, or approximately 10 seconds to reply. The goal here is to have the individual say to you as the doors open at the lobby, "Do you have a few minutes to provide me with more information? I think you can help me." We call this your "elevator pitch." A ten second description of how you can create value for a client. In essence, the elevator pitch is the slogan of your value proposition. An elevator pitch must be worded using "gut English" versus mission statement speak. So it stands to reason that you must develop your value proposition first. Prior to developing the consulting practice of Power Marketing, I began asking people what the word "value" meant to them. I received many different answers. Value, like the words "success" and "beauty," are in the eyes of the beholder. We define value in our own terms.

WHAT IS VALUE?

The value proposition is one of the most misunderstood elements of sales effectiveness. Though it seems simple enough, many sales people think in terms of benefits, but benefits are only part of the equation. There is an equation to buying anything. V = B - C, or Value = Benefits - Costs. There are only two ways to increase your value. The first, which is common in today's highly competitive, global economy is to drop the price, or discount, a practice used often with products or services that have been highly commoditized. The personal computer, the cellular phone, airline fares, discount stock brokers, even legal advice can be purchased at discounted rates. The second way to increase your value is to augment the benefit(s) you bring. The equation of "value = benefit - cost" is based solely on the customer's perception, so the only way to truly bring more benefit to the table is to be more intimate with the customer's business objectives and challenges. Many sales people are trying to understand what the customer needs without really knowing why they need it. The "why" is what we refer to as "business pain." Knowing their pain prepares you to bring the gain, and it isn't exclusively connected to the products or services offered by your company. Advice, insight, contacts, experience, and information from a business savvy professional can make the difference in creating loyal customers for life, & if you are helping your customer solve business problems and/or achieve business objectives, you are creating value. A well understood and customer aligned value proposition will set you apart from your competitors.

WHO RECOGNIZES VALUE?

Let's focus on the person. Who in a company feels the business pain the most? A common mistake is calling too low in an account & we're not talking about the first floor of the building, but about the level of employee in the company. The office manager, the engineering manager, the service manager, the network manager, the manager of computer systems, the administration manager are all nice titles & many sales people are quite happy to spend their time with these individuals, but it's also true that we need to develop many relationships within an account. So let's examine the typical company from a decision making stand point. The following illustration outlines the three levels of a company, the executive, middle management and influencers.

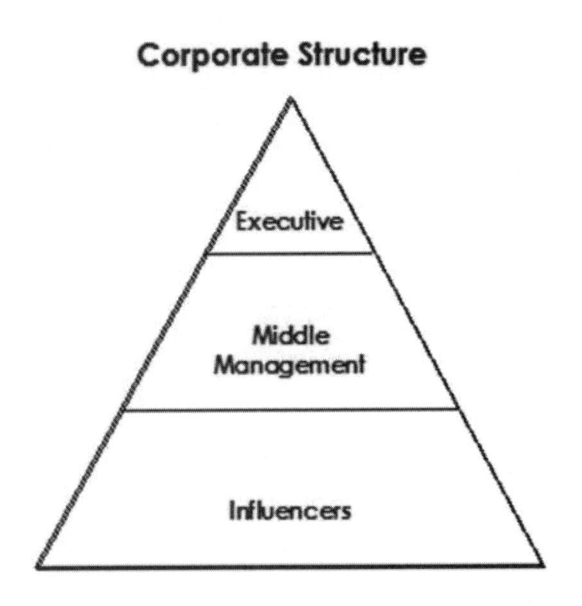

Operations are the tactical implementers of organizations with the titles, office manager, network manager, etc.. They are influencers and influencers rarely make decisions, however they can, and do influence them. To influencers, best price wins, they focus on yesterday, always ready to tell you about policy or procedures. "That's not the way we do things around here" is influencer talk. Their agenda is "knowledge is power" & they think the more they know, the more the company is dependent on them. They want to be seen within the company as the problem solver, the "go to person" & they don't need a "white knight" sales person riding in and getting all the credit, I mean, what would that do to their power? There are usually three kinds of influencers: operational, technical and financial. As sales people, we can't ignore them, however we must recognize them for who they are.

Middle Management concern themselves more with return on investment. Typical middle management talk would be "How can you help me achieve my plan this fiscal year?" They focus on today, & their agenda is different than that of the Influencer. They have already achieved some success within the company and are interested in sustaining that success and attaining more. In the 90's we experienced the global economy taking hold, which forced many companies to downsize or reengineer themselves. The middle management layer was clearly hard hit in terms of thinning the ranks. Again, as sales professionals, we can not limit our customer relationships to middle management.

The executive level of organizations are concerned with measurable results such as increased revenues, stock price, market share, reducing expenses, new advantages on competitors and attracting new customers. They build vision and create business strategy, & their focus is on tomorrow, planning the company's next 5 - 10 years. To them it's not about price, they think in terms of value and how products, services, and people can support their vision and strategy. Personal agenda at this level is highly political, every executive would like to be known as the great leader who has developed a winning company, so the executive level is always open to new ideas and is willing to take calculated risks. After considering these facts, it becomes obvious which level we as sales professionals should be calling.

A value proposition must be presented at the executive level. It will not be recognized at the operational level and only somewhat at middle management levels, so what is a value proposition?

VALUE PROPOSITION DEFINED

"The value your company's products and service have, articulated in your customers terminology, complete with quantifiable business justification". Simply said, "Why do customers do business with you?" Often as companies grow and change, a gap between leadership and field sales develop. The original value the company presented to its clients becomes watered down or even forgotten. Competitive pressures can also contribute to the erosion of your value proposition. There is tangible merit in understanding your value proposition and making it intrinsic in everything you do, so it should be the foundation of your entire selling approach, your marketing materials and message, your delivery and, equally important your attitude. Here are some examples of value propositions in action.

CLIENT PROFILES

In late 1995 Power Marketing conducted a sales and marketing assessment for Kal Tire, a $400m Western Canadian company which provides commercial and retail tire products and services. Kal Tire enjoys a 60% market share in Western Canada with over 140 locations and many loyal customers. A large part of Kal Tire's growth through the late 80's and through the early 90's came through acquisition. Our assessment process involved meeting with the executive management team of Kal

Tire, interviewing their sales managers, sales people and their customers. We then evaluated their value proposition.

Kal Tire executives believed their value proposition was the knowledge of their people. The sales force believed the value they offered the customer was the number of locations, or coverage. But their customers told us their value proposition was that "Kal Tire helped them deliver to their customers, indirectly impacting cash flow and supporting customer satisfaction levels." Many of Kal Tire's customers are in the business of transportation, so they don't get paid if they don't deliver, and if late, customer retention will be a challenge. There was a rather noticeable gap in Kal Tire's value proposition. Kal Tire's slogan is "You'll Like Us For More Than Our Tires". So using the information we gathered from their customers, we gave them a new slogan for their commercial accounts. "Helping You Deliver." Kal Tire is now using this new message in their sales approach and it has made a significant impact.

In 1996, Power Marketing conducted a sales and marketing assessment for a small financial planning and management company in Vancouver called Loney Financial Corporation.

The founder and president Mr. Dan Loney is an excellent consultative sales person, who believed his company's value proposition was their financial planning and investment management expertise. After several interviews with Loney Financials clients, they summarized their value proposition to be "Trust, honesty and integrity." There were references to the strong financial planning expertise and sound investment management, but the most agreed upon items were trust, honesty, and integrity. The second highest component of value was Dan Loney's networking abilities. Dan is a consultative sales person who solves his customers' business problems, & since then Dan has taken action on the discovery of his true value proposition and is now evolving his company logo and image to reflect "trust, honesty and integrity." Well done Dan!

In these examples our clients' customers endorse what was believed to be their value propositions and believe their value has an even greater significance.

But there are other cases where our client's customers strongly disagreed with the internal value proposition our client espoused. In these cases, a different strategy is needed. If you believe you offer value in a certain way but your customers disagree with it, you are wasting your time, money and effort communicating the disagreed value message. Only advertise and promote what the customer believes your value to be. If you want to be known for having more, or different value, you must first earn this reputation, be able to prove it, and then consistently communicate it. Make your customers proud, before you get loud!

ADDING CONSULTATIVE VALUE

Value is not tied to the product or service exclusively. This next section will provide you with a planning tool to help you look at your customers, first through their eyes and then as a consultant. We refer to this exercise as the three rings of consultative selling. Step one in this exercise looks at the small ring in the center of the following illustration. To complete this exercise, we are going to ask you to resign from your current employer, just for the exercise of course. Select an actual customer you are currently working with, and write down the name on the illustration below. This company has just appointed you to their board of directors and if the company succeeds, your stock options will allow you to retire a wealthy individual. You want this company to win. With your director hat on, not your sales hat, ask: What is their vision? What are their goals? What are the business challenges facing this company? What is stopping them from achieving their objectives? In other words, what business issues keep the CEO of this company awake at night? Write down your answers in the center circle.

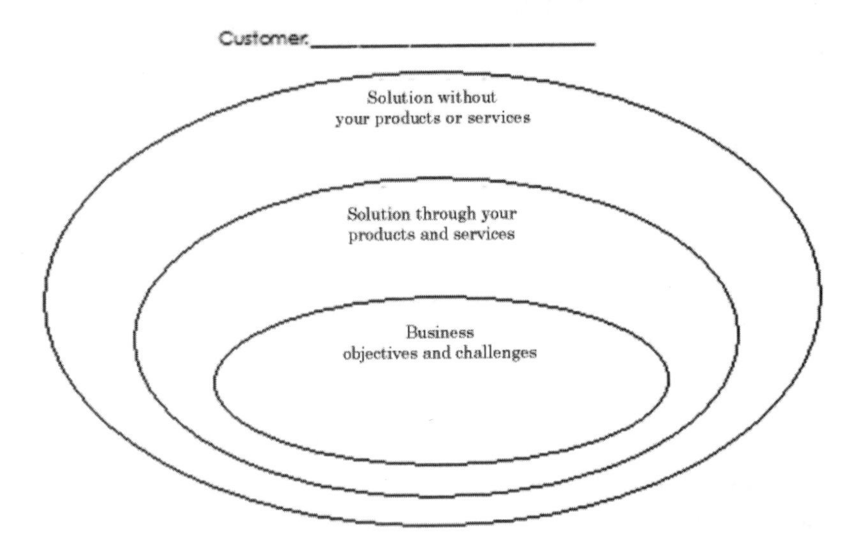

The second step requires you to resign as director and return to your position as a sales person. Using the second ring, with your products and services, can you solve or help to solve the business issues in the center? You can't change the business issue to fit your product or service, as the business needs always drive the solution. Companies don't purchase mainframe computers and then figure out what to use them for. Solve the customer's problems and support their objectives through your products and services, write your answers in the second ring.

"Call high,
Find the pain,
Bring the gain"

The third step requires you to remove your sales hat again, and put on the hat of a business consultant. How can you help to address the objectives and challenges of this company at the executive level? What advice could you offer? What processes could you introduce them to? Has your company overcome challenges that your customer is facing, and if so, could you introduce them to people in your organization that may offer valuable experience? Are there other professionals you know who could help them with their objectives and challenges? Perhaps you could introduce them. Do you have other customers whom this client is targeting or trying to do business with? Again, you could act as a strategist and introducer. Do you have access to information that your customer would find valuable? Think like a business consultant and write in the outer ring concepts for adding value beyond your products and services. The test is that you can not get paid for the outer ring activity or have it prepare to sell your solution. To use a hockey analogy, the outer ring is like getting an assist, not a goal, but the customer still awards you with a point.

Solving customer's business problems and helping them to achieve business objectives through using your products and services is strategic selling. Helping to solve them without getting paid is consultative selling. The equity you are building with the account can be considered an investment on your part. You want to manage how much time you invest, because you need to achieve your own revenue objectives, but when you have developed this kind of relationship with the account, your prices don't have to be the lowest, your products don't have to be the best, your service does not have to be the most responsive. You have the best relationship and you'll keep the account. The test comes when a customer asks you to attend a strategic planning meeting with their senior management team because of the advice and support you have provided them. In fact, they offer to pay for your time. Congratulations! You have arrived as a consultative advisor to this customer. Let's ensure that all of our customers see us this way. Our software SalesLookASP tracks business pain and outer ring value on a deal by deal basis.

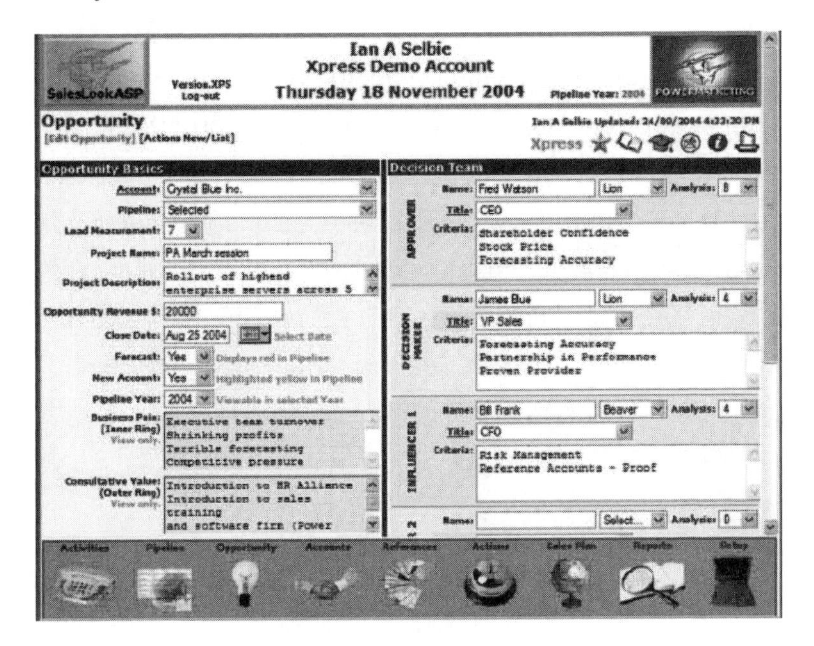

DEVELOPING YOUR VALUE PROPOSITION

In this next section we will examine how to develop your value proposition using Power Marketing as an example. We first viewed our customers as a group. In order to succeed, it is required that we speak as soon as possible to the President, CEO or owner of a company. After establishing contact with the CEO, we then sought to understand their business needs as seen by both the CEO and the Vice President of Sales. We can also be introduced to the company by their Director of Sales or Marketing and develop a relationship at this level.

To develop our value proposition we had to think like customers at these different levels. We asked ourselves: What keeps these individuals awake at night? What do they see as their toughest business challenges? What are their top line objectives? What we are doing here is discovering their "business pain."

Some of you at this point are saying to yourselves, "Fine, I understand, from now on I'm only calling at or near the top, but what do I do with the other twenty accounts where I'm calling too low?" Calling at senior levels is the best way to go, but what about the accounts you have begun relationships with at more junior levels. Do we climb over their heads to get to senior management and risk alienating existing relationships? These existing relationships must be carefully managed, because they too have taken a long time to develop. In many cases going over their heads can backfire and damage your position. Suggest to your point of contact that they are a strategic account or opportunity to your company, and your Vice President, would like to meet with their Vice President to get closer in terms of business objectives and strategic initiatives. This way you are maintaining your relationship, but leveraging your own organization to help you to call higher in the customer's organization.

When developing Power Marketing's value proposition, our second step was to list the services we provide. The third step took time to work through, we compared our list of services to their list of business pain at each level, & where there was a match, we asked ourselves, "How does our particular service address their specific business pain?" We then asked ourselves "Can we quantify our solution?" and "Can we prove it?" After mapping their business pain to our services we had a value proposition for each level we spoke to in our customer's organizations. There are real differences in each level; the following model illustrates how we developed our value proposition.

To help you understand our approach, we have provided you with our blueprint. Though the lines connecting our services with our client's business pains may appear busy or confusing, the following model works. One of our services includes facilitating senior management workshops for our clients, helping them develop their value propositions. This blueprint and approach is what we use.
We have included the value points to the CEO, President, and

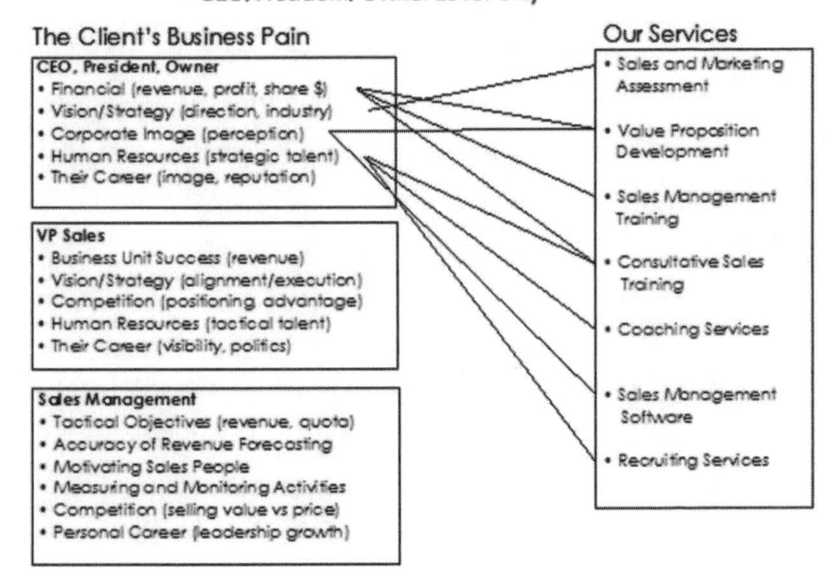

Owner level only. This blueprint gave us a strong understanding of our value proposition.

In the third step, we asked ourselves; "How does our sales and marketing assessment service address the CEO business pain of vision and strategy?" Our answer: "Through our assessment process we will validate whether the vision and strategy is being implemented throughout the sales force and experienced by their customers" but how can we quantify it? This is hard to measure, other than to say "X percent of our clients have either augmented their strategies or changed how they communicate them as a result of experiencing our assessment services." Can we prove it? Yes we can through client reference letters.

Through developing our own value proposition, four benefits emerged. First was a consistent message across our company. We were able to create an elevator pitch that we all agreed upon: "We help our clients achieve their revenue and margin objective through a proven set of sales and marketing services." We usually get asked how, which is exactly the response we want. The second benefit was a revised corporate presentation. We "clientized" our existing one, focusing more on their business pain than on our services. The third benefit was an executive white paper discussing the various business pains of sales organizations today. The ideas we came up with served as the framework for our executive white paper entitled "In Search of Sales Effectiveness." The fourth benefit came in the form of 15 "killer questions" to ask prospective clients. We assembled a needs assessment questionnaire designed to make the clients uncomfortable upon answering our questions. We designed these questions by analyzing the answers to the question: "How does our service address their business pain?" We then convert these answers to questions. For example, our value proposition development services helps ensure the client's corporate image is consistently communicated throughout the sales force. So we came up with the question "How do you ensure that your sales force is confidently representing the complete value your company offers?" Most senior management disliked their answer to this question. We devised 15 "killer questions" based on this principal. There is real value in understanding and consistently communicating your value proposition.

We have provided a template for developing your value proposition. It is critical to follow the right order. First, itemize the business pain of the levels involved from your customers' perspective. To help you validate them, ask your own executive and other functional levels you call on. Second, list your products and services, then map them together one at a time, asking yourself: "Does this product address that line item of business pain? If yes, how? Can you quantify it? Can you prove it?" To keep organized, we recommend copying this template and doing the exercise one level at a time.

We have taken the liberty of leaving in the business pain for CEOs, Presidents and Owners, as their pain can be similar, but how you address it will be unique to you. It took the Power Marketing team more than two days to feel complete with the process of value proposition development. We suggest forming a team within your company of senior management as well as sales & marketing management, and spending at least

Value Proposition Development Template

The Client's Business Pain	Your Solutions
CEO, President, Owner • Financial (revenue, profit, share $) • Vision/Strategy (direction, industry) • Corporate Image (perception) • Human Resources (strategic talent) • Their Career (image, reputation)	

one day trying to complete this template. It will create some very interesting dialog. Have small teams come up with a company elevator pitch and present it to the others. Remember an elevator pitch needs to be humanly speakable, not like mission statements. If you're serious about embracing the value proposition, you should have someone interview your customers objectively. As the earlier case profiles pointed out, what you think your value proposition is and what your customers think it is may be two different things. You don't want to push the wrong message. Once you understand your value proposition it becomes a critical part of your entire sales and marketing strategy. It serves as the framework for dealing with your customers. Your value proposition should be clearly articulated in all sales tools and consistently presented as a part of your sales process. Your sales skills should be developed to confidently communicate your value proposition in a consistent manner, and your sales management should be able to mentor and coach the sales force on all elements of the value proposition. The value proposition is an integral component in the model of sales effectiveness.

VALUE PROPOSITION ASSESSMENT

1. As you understand it today, describe your organization's value proposition. Why do you think customers do business with you?

____

2. To what degree is your organization's value proposition communicated to employees?

- ❑ Poorly
- ❑ Fairly
- ❑ Well
- ❑ Very Well

3. To what degree is your organization's value proposition communicated to customers?

- ❑ Poorly
- ❑ Fairly
- ❑ Well
- ❑ Very Well

4. Describe how your sales force quantifies your value in the eyes of your customer?

____

5. Do your people have the "right tools" to effectively communicate your value proposition?

- ❑ Not at all
- ❑ Partially
- ❑ Somewhat
- ❑ Yes

CHAPTER FOUR

The Sales Process

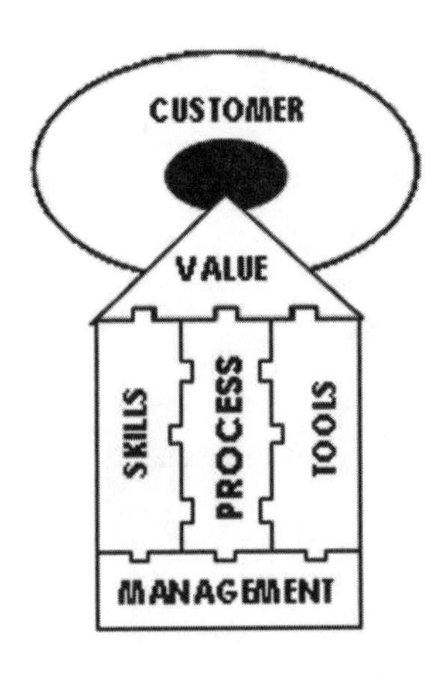

Its 6 am on a Monday morning, the alarm clock sounds and you immediately wake up and proceed to get ready for your day. Your daily ritual includes a shower, getting dressed and having a cup of coffee. You then get in your car and take the fastest possible route to the office and for many of us the drive is virtually identical every day. What we've just described is a process - a process we do 5 days a week and one we've probably all perfected to the point that we are seldom arrive late. The science of identifying prospects, qualifying them, successfully engaging and keeping them is also a process that can be executed in a highly effective manner. We call this the sales process.

DEFINING THE SALES PROCESS

We define the sales process as the required steps from proactively identifying leads, right through to developing and leveraging reference customers. In fact, there is a loop in the sales process, which will become evident later. Before we define the sales process, we must ask why it is important to have one. As we described in previous chapters, Power Marketing performs sales and marketing assessments for its clients. Part of this engagement includes a sales process assessment. During our interviews with our client's sales people and sales managers, we ask them what their sales process is. We normally get a different answer from everyone we ask. This has led us to say there are usually as many sales processes in a company as there are sales people; everyone does it their own way. This creates two very significant challenges for the company. The first challenge relates to the experience of the customer. If each sales person is dealing with his customers his way, it creates a high level of inconsistency with the customers. Depending on who the sales person is, that customer's experience will be based not on the companies process, but on the sales person's. You'd think this would not be the case in larger companies, because they are larger, they would have established a standardized sales process. You may be saying to yourself, "standardize? make me a clone?" Not at all, there is plenty of room for personality, style and character. Having a streamlined set of steps for the sales process only makes sales organizations more effective and increases results. The second challenge of not having a unified sales process is experienced by sales management. We define good sales management as sales leaders who proactively coach and mentor the sales force. In order to mentor someone, they must themselves be highly effective at what they're teaching and coaching, so, they particularly need to understand the steps in the sales process. The sales manager who is leading a sales team of 10 to 15 sales people cannot be effective if he/she has to know 10 to 15 different sales processes. Again, the value of standardizing one "best practice" sales process enables the sales manager to integrate the coaching of his/her sales team.

> **"The root evil in sales today is poor sales process"**

In business-to-business selling, there are at least eight steps in a sales process. For the model of indirect, or selling through a channel, there will be more. We define the eight steps as:

1) Lead identification
2) Position company value proposition
3) Client needs assessment & qualification
4) Create and present proposal
5) Earn client commitment
6) Delivery solution/engagement
7) Proactive account management
8) Leverage reference accounts

To help you put it all in perspective, we have included a copy of Power Marketing's sales process blueprint as a point of reference.

Power Marketing's Sales Process Blueprint

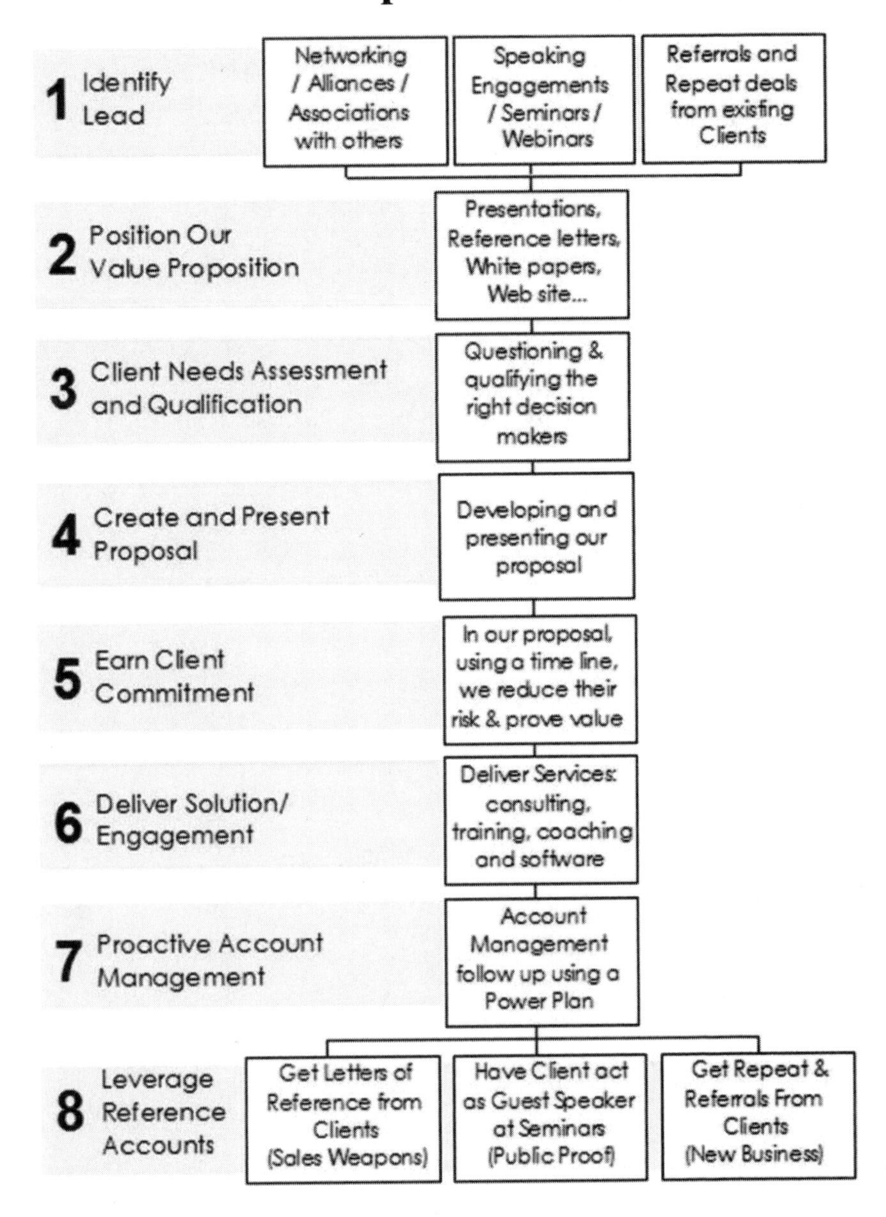

THE EIGHT STEP SALES PROCESS:

1 PROACTIVE LEAD IDENTIFICATION

This step is one of the most inconsistent steps in the average salesperson's process. For many sales people, prospecting is waiting for the phone to ring, and in many companies the phone does ring. However answering the phone or reactive prospecting usually results in the prospect asking you what your price is, because they have taken the initiative and are shopping in the market. Companies who have large advertising budgets and telemarketing departments do provide the sales force with leads and in some cases these can be quality leads. However we still view this as reactive prospecting.

We ask our clients the following questions when assessing their lead identification step in the sales process:
"Where does your most profitable business come from?"
"With which customers do you have the shortest selling cycle?"
"How many repeat opportunities and referrals are you getting from your existing customers?"
"What activities have produced the best revenue results?"
For most companies, the best advertising is word of mouth, referral advertising. This is certainly the case in our business. Ninety-five percent of our clients have come as a result of referrals from existing clients, allies, or contacts from within our network. Do we still cold call? Yes! Do we still host seminars? Yes! Do we still take on speaking engagements? Yes! Do we send out targeted direct mail? Yes! Later in this chapter, we will introduce an opportunity management tool entitled "The Opportunity Pipeline." The pipeline is used by

sales people and sales managers to focus, plan and manage all the deals they are working on. The first phase of the pipeline is "Activities." What activities are we proactively engaging in, to generate interested prospects for the pipeline? Some activities include: account management meetings with existing customers, 10 phone calls per week to a targeted list not already in the pipeline, seminars/briefings/workshops/networking events/ associations/clubs and direct mail campaigns with telephone follow up. These are all proactive activities.

When a sales person gets a lead, what priority do they put on pursuing the lead? Sales people are usually very busy and following up on leads can take a back seat to other steps in the sales process. However, successful sales people realize that to sustain their success, they need a steady flow of new prospects to keep their pipelines full. Our advice to sales people is clearly "keep the prospecting tap turned on."

2 POSITION COMPANY VALUE PROPOSITION

Once a lead has been positively identified, the sales person will schedule a meeting with the prospective customer. Another classic mistake sales people make is in meeting with anyone who'll give them the time of day. In the value proposition chapter, we discuss the corporate structure and decision making levels of organizations. This first contact with the prospect should be a meeting with someone at the executive or senior management level of the prospects organization. As mentioned, trying to climb the ladder later on can be very challenging. This first meeting is with an executive. I usually begin a meeting with a president or vice-president by saying "what I would like to cover with you today is to get a clear understanding of your business challenges. I'd also like to explain our company and services, and explore the merits of a complementing fit." In the case of a first time meeting, the person is likely to suggest that I go ahead and explain what we do, which is the "position company value proposition" step of the sales process.

In the value proposition chapter, we speak about knowing your value and developing a presentation tool that helps the sales force consistently and effectively communicate it. We refer to this as your pitch. An effective pitch can range from six to twelve slides that help you briefly describe your company, your services, the business pain you address, and include a list of existing customers as proof sources. Your pitch can be in the form of a color, computer projected slide presentation, color or black and white overhead transparencies, or even an eight and half by eleven, black and white print of these slides. In fact on a daily basis at Power Marketing, we use a colour printed version of our pitch. We have found this format works very well for one-on-one meetings in offices or at restaurants! One of the beauties of having your pitch in this printed form is that it is very easy to makes changes and inexpensive to produce.

There are other tools that can help you position your company's value proposition, such as white papers and letters of reference, which we will talk about in detail in the sales tools and weapons chapter.

3 CLIENT NEEDS ASSESSMENT & QUALIFICATION

The client needs assessment and qualification step is absolutely critical. We are often invited in by presidents of companies and asked: "My sales force means well, but if they only knew how to close the deal, our revenues would really be impressive. Can you teach them how to close?" On every assessment we have done, we discover it is never a closing issue. It is always failure in doing due diligence in the needs assessment, and qualification step of the process. It's not about closing; it's all about qualifying! To conduct an effective client needs assessment and qualify an opportunity, we must ask questions on three levels. The first is the business level. Our objective here is to establish credibility as not just another sales person trying to close him, but rather a business consultant who understands his industry, company, competition and current company events and initiatives. We are attempting to create executive currency and identify business pain. Executives love to talk about their company and themselves, so the consultative sales person needs to know the right questions to ask in order to initiate this dialogue. A few of my personal favorites to begin an executive meeting are:

"How are today's business challenges affecting your company's ability to achieve your goals?"

"What are the most critical business challenges facing your company over the next two years?"

"If you could easily change three things about your company to help you achieve your objectives, what would they be?"

As mentioned, we are looking for business pain, since anything that would help address the business pain as perceived by the executive has value. The objective of the second level of questioning is to create awareness and urgency on their business pain that our distinct services address. In the value proposition chapter we discuss coming up with your "killer questions." At Power Marketing we have developed a library of fifteen, and on a regular basis, I use 5 or 6 of them. Along with this objective, we are learning about their real needs. The third level of questioning is entirely committed to qualifying the opportunity. As sales people, all we really have is our time. Rather than chasing opportunities blindly, we need to selectively pick our battles. We as sales people must determine if we want to pursue this opportunity, which means investing time, energy and resources on it. Who makes the first decision? The customer? No, it's you, the sales person.

Therefore on the first call we want to understand the following:

- ❑ What is their business pain?
- ❑ What are their specific needs that I can address through our products and services?
- ❑ What are their specific needs that I may be able to address without our products and services?
- ❑ Who are all the individuals involved in making this decision?
- ❑ What is the approved budget for this project?
- ❑ What are the internal costs associated with not solving this problem?
- ❑ What is the established time line for solving this problem? Why?
- ❑ Who are my competitors and are you already doing business with any of them?

- ❑ Do you see a complementing fit for our services in your organization?

Here are three things to consider on the first call: (1) did you leave with enough information to create a proposal, (2) did you leave a distinctive impression that communicated your value proposition effectively and (3) did you sell yourself?

CREATE AND PRESENT PROPOSAL

4

When a prospect asks for a proposal too quickly, heads up! I always say, "We are very interested in your business and will certainly develop a proposal for you. However in order to serve both our best interests, I need to learn more about your company and your needs. Is there anyone else whose input is required at this point?" After asking my questions and gathering the information I need to create the proposal, I always ask the prospect when could we get together next to go through the proposal. If the prospect says, "Just send it or fax it to me," I say no. We must go through it together, because discussion is always required. If we are not calling at the right level and all we do is send it or fax it, we are trusting someone within the prospect's organization to do our work for us. Is this person a sales person? Do they know your company and solution intimately? Are they able to handle objections as they arise? Do they have your understanding of the many other customers you have served? We must present our proposal in person to the people making the decision. We should have conducted a needs assessment with all the people involved in making the decision. In some cases, usually in Government, their procurement process may preclude you from doing a proposal presentation, because they may have issued an RFP (request for proposal).

For most businesses, 70 to 80 percent of the content of all proposals is the same. If you haven't already, we'd recommend creating a standard proposal template to act as a starting point for the entire sales team. For far too many sales people, the proposal is really only a quotation, with product numbers and prices. A real proposal must start with your understanding of the prospect's business challenges and objectives. Putting this in writing has major significance, as it frames our understanding of their situation. When presenting our proposal we start with this section. If our understanding is slightly off, this gives us a chance to adjust our proposal with the prospect which is another reason that proposals must be presented in person. If the prospect has never done business with you before, we recommend that the proposal also include letters of reference from other customers. A proposal should include the following components: cover letter, table of contents, prospect's business challenges & objectives, your company profile, product/service/engagement description, pricing information, terms and time lines, list of existing customers and appropriate letters of reference.

You company image and professionalism are very important. Always have someone proof read your proposal, even after your computer has spell checked it. Something that is very important to consider is how you package your proposal. There are many ways of doing this, from stapled letterhead, put into a company folder, to letterhead run through a binding machine. All the people on the sales team should standardize on a packaging method. Consistency is critical in terms of projecting a professional image. The presentation of the proposal is so important because if the short listed companies have similar solutions with similar value, often the presentation itself can win the deal. When presenting your proposal, start with your understanding of the prospect's business challenges and objectives. Follow the format you used in writing the proposal. Depending on the opportunity size, I will often build a few Power Point slides or put them on overheads. A set of slides can help the presenter communicate his message clearly and succinctly. Your presentation also shows the prospect that you have gone to quite a bit of trouble to earn their business.

5 EARN CLIENT COMMITMENT

For many sales people they put a proposal or quote together, fax it into the prospect and wait for the prospect to call them. Their attitude is "you win some, you lose some." This often becomes "lose many." Earning the prospect's business could also be called closing, however, focusing on the close is a trap. As mentioned earlier in this chapter, sales people don't have a problem closing, they have a problem qualifying. If we do a diligent job of qualifying, earning the customer's commitment comes naturally. When you buy something, a house, a car, a computer, do you like the sales person to try and close you? In fact, the harder they push, the further away you want to go.

I mentioned time line, in the create and present proposal phase. The time line can be a useful tool in helping you stay close to the prospect along the road to decision. To create a time line, you must first understand when the prospect would like to have the solution in place. Then work backwards in terms of any preparation they must do to prepare for the solution being put in place. Consider any other lead times that must be considered from the suppliers, and then the decision time required by the team of people within the prospect's organization. A time line can be a tool to help both you and the prospect stay focused and organized.

If you have already been doing business with the customer and the proposal is for a repeat order or other products or services your company offers, you should already have a good working relationship with the account. However if your proposal is to a company that you have not dealt with before, we recommend finding ways to reduce their risk in giving your company a try. There are three ways to reduce the risk for the prospect. The first, and we did talk about it already, is to offer the prospect reference letters and a chance to speak with existing customers. The second way is to offer a guarantee. Depending on the product or service a 100% money back guarantee may not be possible, however consider a risk/reward guarantee. If the customer is not fully satisfied with the product or service they only pay a percentage of the price: 60%, 70% or 80%. If satisfied, 100%. In fact if your product or service exceeds the customer's expectations, suggest that they can pay you more, at their own discretion. The third method for reducing the prospect's risk is to offer some kind of trial or evaluation prior to making a full commitment. When I was at Apple Computer,

I used the trial method to open a very large corporate account that later went on to purchase in excess of $12M of Macintosh computers in four years.

When you have qualified an opportunity, you've presented your proposal and you are on the short list and waiting for their decision. Should you be staying in touch with the prospect? My answer is yes. You'll want to be sensitive on how often; ask them how often they would like you to stay in touch with them. When a prospect does not return your calls, or goes quiet on you, it usually is not a good sign. They are usually talking to your competition. Be positive, proactive and persistent, but don't be a pest.

6 DELIVERY SOLUTION/ENGAGEMENT

When we win a deal, the party is on……especially if its a big deal. When winning, we usually don't examine why we won. When we lose a deal most sales people are upset, some of us actually get mad, but few of us ask for a meeting with the lost customer to be debriefed on why we lost. The objective is to learn how we might win their business next time. You may even be able to salvage the deal based on your professionalism and attitude to learn.

For most sales organizations, the sales person's role, as it has been explained to them, is to find the customers and pass them onto others in the organization who will be responsible for delivering the products and/or services. The salesperson should stay involved from a coordinating point of view. They should not be involved in every detail, but they should keep the customer informed on status and other communication details. Many customers have their biggest problems with companies when they actually buy something. It is during that moment of truth when great sales people separate themselves from the average to good sales people, ensuring that the customer's expectations are delivered on. Great sales people translate this to "Is my word worth anything?" Problems do occur, it is not a perfect world and there will be issues. The way that great sales people react during these moments of truth sets them apart. Tell your customers the truth! And tell them often!

7 PROACTIVE ACCOUNT MANAGEMENT

As mentioned in the previous paragraph, many sales people think their job is over with the customer as soon as they sign them up. Here's some research that supports our position. If it costs you $700 to develop a new customer, it will only cost $100 to get a repeat order from an existing customer. I realize that in some industries the repeat order may take 5 to 10 years to get, but here are four excellent reasons to follow up on a regular basis. The first is to ensure that they are happy with your product or service. When you purchase something on a personal basis, be it a house, car, computer or furniture, and you are happy with the value you receive and the way in which you were dealt with, you will tell 3 or 4 people. But if you are not satisfied with the product, service or the way you are dealt with you'll tell 10 or more people. Think about every customer you have, what are they saying to their colleagues, associates and friends about you. The second reason you want to follow up on a regular basis, is to earn a letter of reference. When someone puts in writing they are happy with your value and with you, they are indirectly saying they will continue to do business with you. This is good, and what's better is using these letters of reference proactively in your sales process. At Power Marketing, we color copy every letter we earn from our clients and distribute them to our sales force and associates. We use them on every sales call to reduce risk and develop confidence in the prospective customer. When creating and presenting our proposals, we include copies from our reference letter library that are relevant to the prospective customer. A Great way to utilize the customers who have provided us with letters, is to ask them to take calls from prospective customers. An existing customer is the most powerful tool any sales person has.

The third reason we want to follow up with our existing customers involves tracking our customer's changing business pain and how we may be able to play a role in solving it. In the Value Proposition Chapter we talk about the three circles. In the center circle we are tracking and understanding the customer's business pain. The second circle helps us to map our solutions to the customer's business pain and the third and largest circle includes other ways we can add value to the customer without selling them anything.

By keeping a regular dialog with our existing customers, we are able to help them address their business pain and sometimes provide them with more solutions, thus earning repeat business from customers.
The fourth reason for follow up with the customer is to receive

referrals to other opportunities, both internal to the customer, and external. As you develop a trusted relationship with your customer, they will become comfortable in providing you with names of people and companies that your products and services

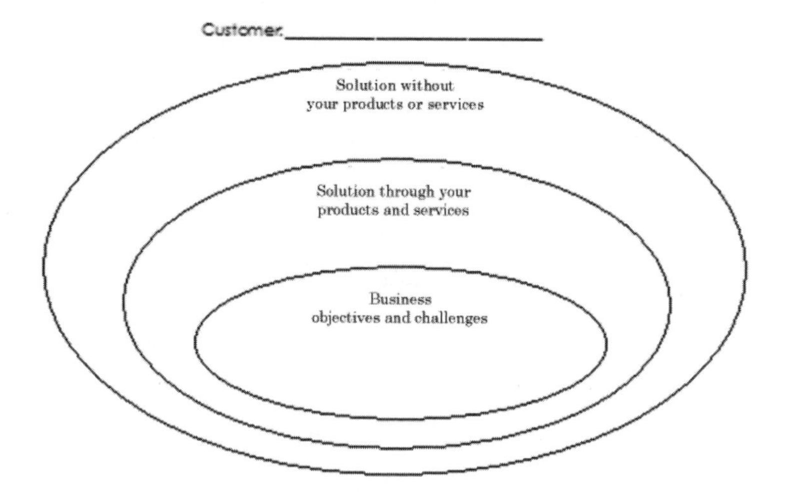

can address. This is earned, and only asked for at the right time. When the customer is happy with your company's solutions and how you have been looking after their needs, and have already provided you with a letter of reference, then they are ready to ask for referrals.

Proactive account management requires discipline and work. If you have 15 existing customers, you will need to manage your time effectively. Perhaps with the smaller customers you may conduct an account planning session on an annual basis. With mid sized accounts, perhaps twice a year, and large accounts on a quarterly basis. Proactive means you'll initiate the meetings, and the objective of the account planning session from the customer's perspective is to ensure they are satisfied with your company's products, services, and people. You will want to track issues and projects outstanding and plan for future work together. There are five steps in proactive account management. The first is setting up the meeting which will include the key individuals from the customer and key individuals from your organization. The second step is to perform a business review at the meeting which includes a look back at business already done together and identifying any outstanding issues that need action. The third step is to contain the current situation. There may be current projects or business in progress that should be recognized and a status report provided by both the customer and your company. The forth step is to investigate the future. Are there any new initiatives or projects pending? Have there been any significant changes within your customer's organization? Has their business pain shifted? How can you and your company address the new business pain or needs of your customer? The fifth step is to document the account planning session and provide everyone at the meeting with a copy of the brief report. This report will have issues and commitments which will need to be delivered on. You might say that account management is really accountability management.

8 LEVERAGE REFERENCE ACCOUNTS

We have already talked about some of the ways to leverage our reference accounts. The letter of reference is an excellent vehicle and having customers take phone calls from prospects is another leverage mechanism. Many companies today are utilizing technology as sales tools which we will discuss in the Sales Tools Chapter. A very effective way to leverage customers using technology is to video some of your happy customers who have experienced great value from your products and services. These video interviews can be edited into a corporate video presentation, and used as a great sales tool, as well as being used in seminars and on your web site. One of the best activities for developing new business is the seminar. A brilliant way to leverage your customers, is to have one or two of them act as guest speakers, which can have an incredible effect on the outcome of your seminar. Some companies have put a catalog of references together which are a number of case profiles, usually sorted by industry, and is yet another way to leverage your existing successes. If you're using computers, consider scanning your reference letters into a computer database making them accessible to the entire sales force.

MANAGING THE SALES PROCESS

How many deals is the average sales person pursuing at any one time? 10? 20? or even 30? Keeping track of these deals at the different stages within the sales process can be an incredible challenge. In our experience, some sales people use the file folder system with the hottest deals at the top of the stack. Some keep track of their deals in their planner, while others have them hidden in their computers on spreadsheets or contact managers. Did I mention that all of these sales people work for the same company? Sound like a forecasting nightmare? How accurate are your sales forecasts? Most companies really struggle with forecasting and one of the reasons is a lack of sales process and reporting consistency within the sales force. This is what led us to create the Opportunity Pipeline. This visual sales and sales management planning and coaching tool provides the sales force with a daily focus on their entire sales world. There are specific business rules for every phase in the pipeline which are consistent with the steps in the sales process. There are usually three areas of weakness for most sales people. The first area is not enough proactive activity coming into the pipeline. The second is failure to qualify opportunities, and thirdly, not leveraging their reference accounts, which is the easiest to correct.

THE OPPORTUNITY PIPELINE

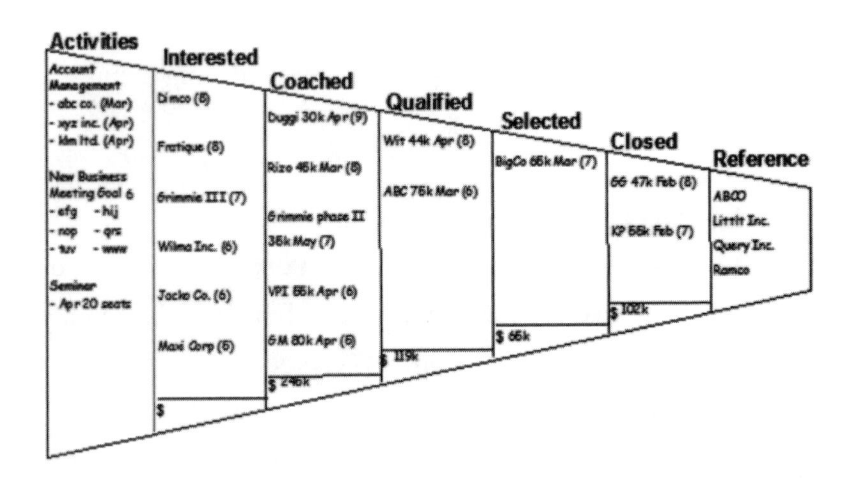

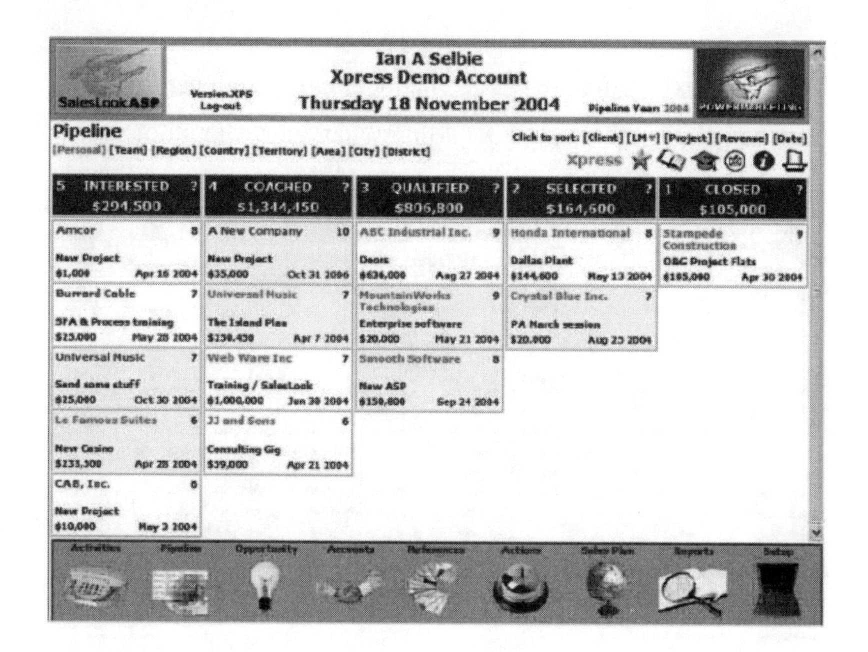

From a sales manager's perspective, the opportunity pipeline is an excellent tool for coaching, forecasting and sales force accountability as displayed above in a screen from our software SalesLookASP.

With a visual glance, the sales manager can get an accurate and very revealing view of who's doing what, and who's not.

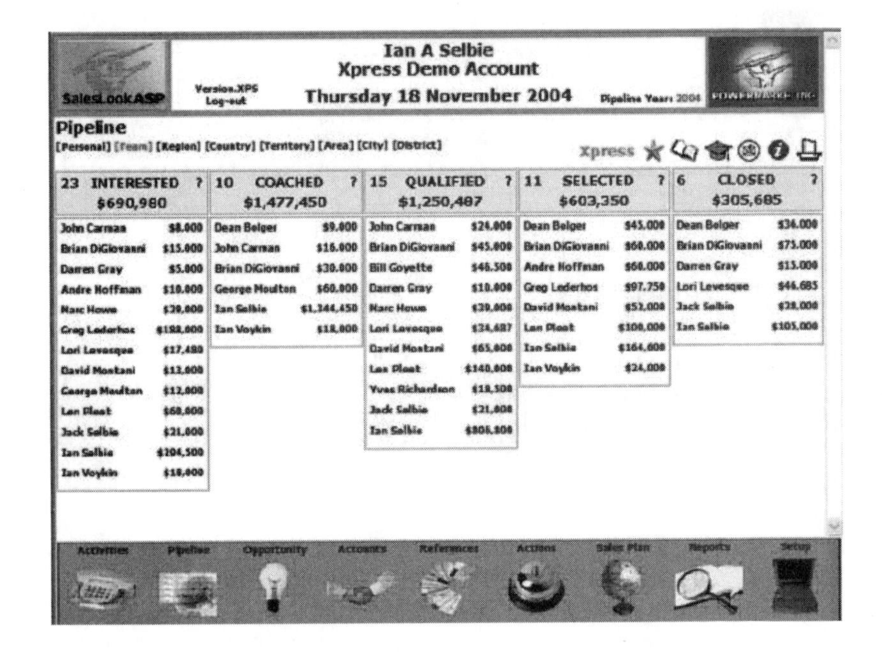

SalesLookASP, is a completely automated, web-based version of our pipeline methodology. Details at www.powermarketingworld.com.

SALES PROCESS ASSESSMENT

1. When performing sales & marketing assessments for our clients we find as many sales processes in a company as there are sales people. How many sales processes do you have in your company

____

2. When you lose deals, where in your existing sales processes does the failure usually occur?

____

3. How effective is your sales management at coaching the sales force with their sales processes?

- ❑ Poor
- ❑ Fair
- ❑ Somewhat effective
- ❑ Very effective

4. How might your sales process be improved?

____

5. How accurate is your sales force at forecasting revenues?

- ❑ Darts anyone?
- ❑ Poor
- ❑ Fair
- ❑ Accurate

CHAPTER FIVE

Consultative Skills for Success

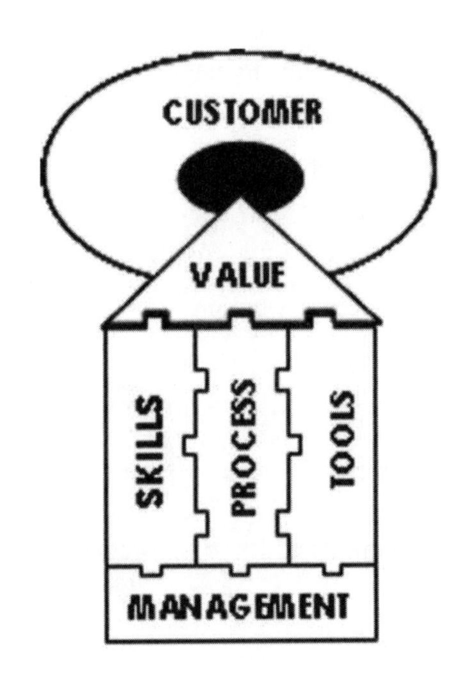

Riding a bike, driving a car and using a computer all require a set of skills. Let's take a brief look at learning how to ride a bike. One of our parents sat us down and told us what we had to do, took us out and showed us how, and then came that scary moment when they pushed us down the street holding on to the back of the bike and finally letting us go. Shortly after for some of us, we were laying on the ground crying and our parents made us feel better by encouraging us to do it again. But the basic principles of learning were all present. We had it explained to us, had it demonstrated to us, we tried it and we got some feedback on it.

There was also something else present that is worth pointing out. We all wanted to ride the bike. This drive is critical in developing sales skills.
I am often asked "what makes a great sales person?" We normally take two full days in our consultative sales training program to answer this question. Over time, I have been able to net it down to three things: confidence, organization and persistence.

CONFIDENCE, ORGANIZATION & PERSISTENCE

Confidence is a key element. When you're looking to buy anything, wouldn't you rather deal with someone who is confident about himself, his company and his products and/or services? Developing confidence is critical for success in a career as a consultative sales person. Heads up, as there is a huge difference between confidence and cockiness. When you are buying something, and the sales person is cocky versus confident what do you want to do? Well my answer is leave, hang up or press "Eject"! More on how to develop confidence in the sales management chapter.

What does being organized mean? Given today's right sized company profile, this usually results in a sales force that needs to "do more with less." Each sales person must look after more customers than they once had to, while ensuring they still dedicate enough time for developing new customers (hunting) Therefore being organized has never been more important. I have heard many sales people tell me they need to improve their time management skills. I believe it's really an issue of priority management. Very seldom can you actually say that you have done everything that should be done. That would be utopia because there is always something else you could do. You must prioritize dynamically to the point where you can always answer the question: "What is the best thing I should do right now" Start by focusing on the most critical. What do I mean by critical? To answer this question, I must define the job description of a sales person. In order of priority, Revenue, Relationships and Reporting. The question can always be answered by reviewing these three points. A sales person's number one job is to create revenue for the company. If there were only two hours left in a week and a sales person had a choice of making a sales call on a prospect who is interested in his products and/or services, or visiting an existing customer or completing his forecast or his pipeline report, what should he do? Do the prospect meeting, and get the forecast/pipeline report done at night if he has to.

Getting organized is one thing, staying organized is another. In the sales process chapter we discussed the importance of having a standard, replicatable sales process. Simply said it's a sales blueprint for success. A tool we have developed to help sales organizations be consistent with their sales process and focus their priorities, is the opportunity pipeline. How many customers does the average sales person in your company look after? How many prospects is the average sales person in your company pursuing at any given time? At what stage are the prospects? How does all this information get tracked? Do things ever fall between the cracks? The opportunity pipeline can be a sales person's best friend, helping him stay organized and focused.

1. **Revenue**
2. **Relationships**
3. **Reporting**

When it comes to persistence, I wish there was a pill or a program to create it, but there isn't! In the Sales Management chapter, we discuss coaching hints that help sales people to be persistent. What criteria about a lead, causes an average sales person to prioritize their time? In our experience, it usually comes down to the biggest deal he's working on. However it may also be the most competitive deal he's working on, or the most complex, or the least profitable, or the slowest at making a decision. To help sales people prioritize their efforts we have developed a practical tool that is tailorable for every company. We call it the "lead measure system." Our clients use it in conjunction with the opportunity pipeline. At Power Marketing, the lead measurement system drives our entire focus and results. Again the concept is to keep it simple, thus being able to quickly assign a rating of 10 for each lead or prospect you are working on. Think about your business: What are the five measuring criteria you use to define the right kind of customers? Profitability, revenue size, differentiation, segmentation, and level of contact, competition, source of lead?

LEAD MEASUREMENT SYSTEM

The system below is utilized differently by all our customers. To serve as an example, the metrics used below are specific to selling Power Marketing services.

1) Source of lead... (Where did we get the lead from?)

- external/executive	2
- internal/non executive	1
- cold call/not endorsed	0

2) Level of contact... (Who is our contact?)

- CEO/President/Owner	2
- VP Sales or Marketing	1
- other	0

3) Location of decision... (Where is the decision made?)

- a city where we have a presence	2
- location with budget autonomy	1
- other	0

4) Size of deal... (Total revenue)

- 100k+ potential	2
- 50K to 100K potential	1
- less than 50K potential	0

5) Competitive Loyalty... (Relationships)

- Pro Power	2
- Neutral	1
- Pro Competitor	0

Using this simple tool, we are quickly able to determine how to prioritize our effort. We help our clients come up with their scoreboard for lead measurement. For the system I mentioned, we use the following scoreboard:

- 10 or 9 points - excellent opportunity, our top priority
- 8 or 7 - good opportunity, next priority
- 6 or 5 - fair opportunity, some risk, can we improve the score with some work?
- 4 or less - poor opportunity, don't give it anymore time... punt! fold em!

We suggest you develop your own lead measurement system and scoreboard. Then test a number of your existing wins, losses and prospects using the system. This will help you come up with a realistic scoring elements and measures.

When using the lead measurement system with the pipeline, you write the lead measure right beside the deals on the pipeline. In fact we recommend that you stack prioritize them using the lead measurement number as follows:

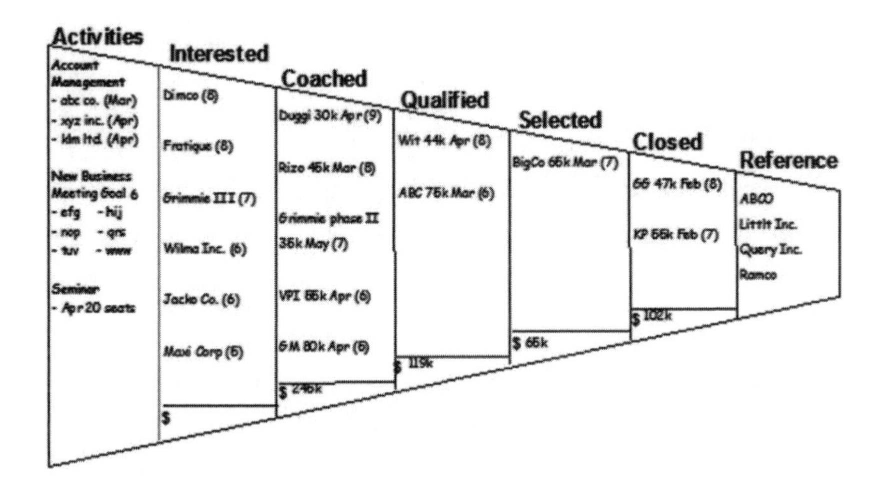

This same lead measurement view of the pipeline is the default view within Power Marketing's software, SalesLookASP.

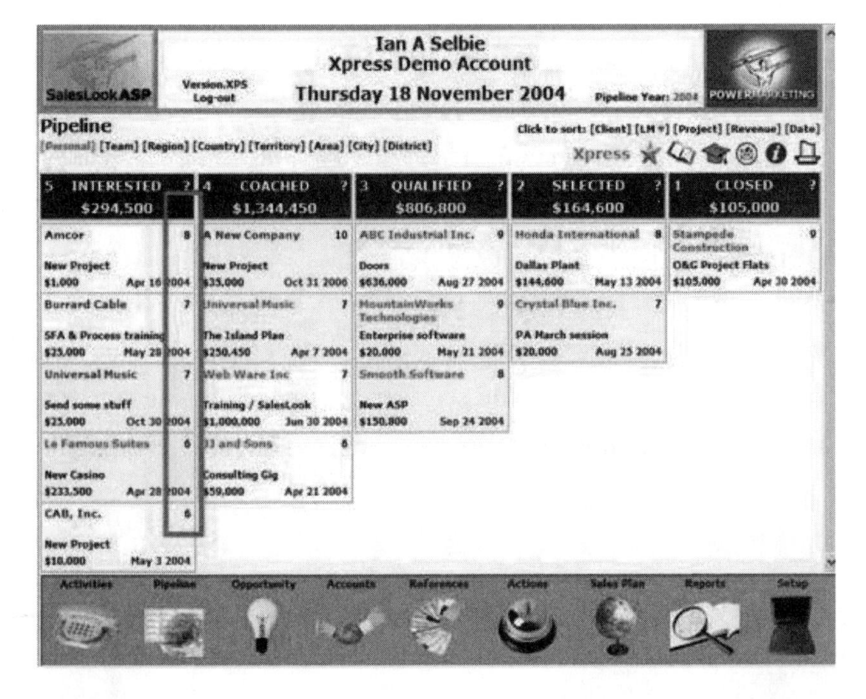

COMMUNICATION SKILLS

Regardless of your position in business, excellent communication skills are essential for true success. In a survey conducted across the US, successful entrepreneurs and sales professionals with incomes over $250k per year were asked what qualities contributed to their success. The results of this survey are as follows:

Top Ten Success Factors For Incomes Over $250,000

1. Communication skills	71%
2. Intelligence	64%
3. Integrity	54%
4. Experience	50%
5. Enthusiasm	46%
6. Self-esteem/attitude	37%
7. Risk-taking/confidence	37%
8. Formal education	29%
9. Ambition	25%
10. Emotional maturity	16%

The three skills of communication are listening, questioning and presenting. Let's examine them starting with listening. Listening skills are a sales person's greatest asset. Please note that listening and hearing are two different things. Have you ever had a meeting with a customer who is explaining his/her situation to you, and instead of listening and understanding, you mentally begin to prepare your next statement? In fact you were probably thinking to yourself... "As soon as he/she shuts up, I'm going to say @#&%&#..." Meanwhile the customer could have been giving you the "keys to the account" but you stopped listening. It's as if someone told sales people that if nobody's speaking, it's their job to fill in the space. Wrong! If nobody is speaking, what's happening? We're both thinking, which is great. If you don't speak, who must? A simple rule of thumb for all sales people is God gave us all two ears and one mouth; all we have to do is use them that way.

Questioning is also critical in understanding a customer's needs, pain, situation, personal agenda and decision process.

There are three levels of questioning.

1) Situational questioning. To determine the customer's business situation, their environment, status of existing suppliers, volumes and quantities.
2) Qualification questioning. To determine whether there is a real opportunity to pursue, decision team, decision criteria, time line, budget, pain and competitors.
3) Killer questions. To create in a customer an awareness of their pain, to create urgency on their pain and to position your company as the provider of the solution.

Presentation skills are also important. A presentation can range from a one-on-one meeting to a large audience, perhaps in a seminar setting, where you may be presenting to hundreds of people. There are some fabulous training programs that address presenting specifically, and we recommend ongoing development and refinement of these important skills. We will provide a few tips on presenting.
When doing a presentation there are three knows:

1) Know your objective... what are you're trying to do as a result of the presentation?

2) Know your audience... who will be attending; what's important to them?

3) Know your content... confident presenters know their stuff cold!

When a presenter gets up and does his presentation, most begin by describing their company, their revenues, their products, their services, me me me! When presenting to a group, start by articulating your understanding of the audience's business situation, their challenges, their needs, and their pain. Then describe how your product and/or services address their needs. We call this earning the right. This understanding should be a part of presentations and proposals. If you are doing a large presentation or seminar, a great way to create credibility with your audience is to utilize an existing customer as a guest speaker. The most powerful tool a sales person has, is proof, and of course the use of technology to help you make your point. It doesn't cut it to show up with overhead transparencies printed in a very small font. Most notebook computers will connect to electronic data projectors, therefore using software such as Microsoft's Power Point it is easy to develop and deliver highly effective and visually rich presentations. It has been said that if the products and prices are very similar, then usually the best presentation wins!

RELATIONSHIP SKILLS

Think about all of the relationships in your life: parents, significant other, siblings, friends, peers, employees and your manager. Strong relationships are based on trust, honesty, integrity, two-way open communications and mutual respect. A relationship with a customer is no different. Customers can be customers for life if the relationship is managed effectively. During my ten years with Apple Computer, I adopted one of Apple's corporate accounts, British Columbia Automobile Association or BCAA. The Vice President of Finance and Chief Information Officer was a gentleman by the name of Roger Smith. After handling their account for two years, Roger and I had developed a relationship based on trust, respect and integrity. I recall a pivotal point in our relationship when I hosted Roger and four of his staff in Cupertino, California (Apple headquarters) at an executive briefing. It was common for Apple to bring strategic accounts to headquarters to show them future products and directions, helping the customer make strategic technology decisions. The executive briefing staff of Apple were excellent at putting together an ideal setting, coordinating the most appropriate Apple resources to present and ensure we addressed the customer's business objectives. Bravo Maria and Mae!!! The BCAA briefing I'm referring to took place in 1988. We were trying to position Apple's servers as a solution to the client/server environment BCAA were developing. We were also positioning our desktop computers, which BCAA were already committed to. Three weeks after we returned from the briefing, Apple announced a special program to US corporate accounts. They were offering three desktop models for the price of two for a short time period. Apple was getting ready to launch a new model and wanted to clear our old inventory. BCAA had purchased 300 units of the previous model 60 days prior to this special offer. I was in shock, because it had not been mentioned at the briefing in Cupertino. Knowing what this would do to the relationship between BCAA and Apple, and more importantly the relationship between Roger and myself, I asked Roger what he wanted me to do. His immediate reaction was predicable. He wanted 1/3 of his money back from the purchase of 300 units. I knew Apple would not go for that but I also knew that BCAA needed more desktop units. Roger agreed that I try to get some free units from Apple. He wanted 40 at no charge, and in the end I was able to get him 25 and some software for free. The bottom line was that Roger was happy knowing I had done my best to save the relationship. After I left Apple, I joined Sybase, a database software company. Sixty days into my tenure with Sybase, BCAA purchased Sybase software from me. After a year I realizing that Sybase was not the company for me, and accepting the Sales Managers position at SHL Systemshouse. Shortly into my tenure with SHL, BCAA became an SHL services account. My point is that customers can be customers for life.

Developing relationships is essential to sales people. This can be challenging given the fact that people are very different. Personality styles are, however, somewhat measurable. Using basic psychology, it is possible to map people's character styles. There are some highly accurate, clinical processes for determining character styles, but in the world of selling, they are mostly impractical. Sales people need a simple process, so we have adopted some basic psychology to help. We analyze two things: dominance and formality. By taking a look at how dominate a person is and how formal they are, the answers to these two questions tell us volumes about a person. Let's try the model on you.

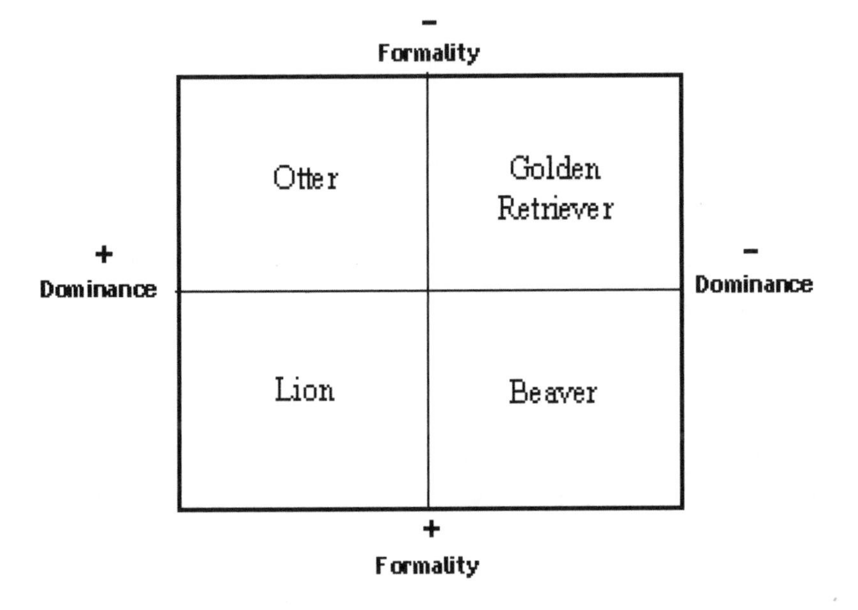

Using the grid above, identify your dominance by plotting a dot on the dominance line. Think about all your relationships. Are you usually more or less dominate and to what degree? Second, identify how formal you are by plotting a dot on the formality line. Think about your desk at work, your walk-in closet, etc. Are you usually on time or late for meetings? The next step is to join the dots, meeting in one of the four quadrants.

Now that you have connected your dots by joining them in one of the four quadrants, turn the page and read about yourself. The four quadrants are appropriately named; Otter, Golden Retriever, Beaver and Lion.

Profile of the Otter:

Why an otter? These people love to play, truly enjoy having fun and are usually the life of the party. They are highly creative and full of energy. They want to create, not conform. They're theme song is... "I did it my way." Otters are very happy when they're in the spotlight. However all four types have pros and cons. The cons on the otter are that because they're easily bored, staying focused is not their strong suit. Thus they will put things on hold in order to pursue more exciting, adventuresome endeavors. They have a number of incompletes or projects not finished yet. To an otter, a watch is jewelry therefore being on time is not always important. Sound like anyone you know?

Profile of the Golden Retriever:

Why a Golden Retriever? If you want a friend for life, find yourself a golden retriever. They are the most loyal people on the planet. They are caring, giving, sharing people, who really like to help others. They are sensitive and care about how people feel. They defend their friends 100% of the time. For all of these positive attributes, the golden retriever also has some cons. Because they spend a lot of their time helping others, they may feel sorry for themselves, especially if nobody helps them. Again, sound like anyone you know?

Profile of the Beaver:

Why a Beaver? These are very busy people, always "working on the dam." The beaver is organized and never forget commitments. An average person may have a "to do" list; a beaver may have a master list of all of their "to do" lists. They are detail and process oriented. They take their time when making decisions and don't like taking risks. But if you want something done right, let a beaver do it. It may take a little longer, but it will be done right the first time. The cons, well because a beaver takes a while to make a decision and the process they go through to reduce the risk is so complete, once they have made their decision they can not be convinced otherwise, thus they can seem inflexible and rigid.

Profile of the Lion:

Why a Lion? Well this one is obvious: lions don't ask for control, they take it. They are King or Queen of the jungle, they need control! They love to start their day with a "to do" list and their favorite thing to do is tick the boxes beside the activities they complete. They love results and are quick to move things out of their way when it comes to getting results. They are impatient; in fact when their parents told them "You need to develop patience in life," they were quick to respond, "If I wanted patients, I would have been a doctor!" This is a personal experience, because I am a lion. The cons, well all through a lion's life, we have been accused of being self centered and selfish, to which we have responded, "so what's your point?" Yes, we lions are insensitive. Our software SalesLookASP tracks the character style of the decision makers of every opportunity.

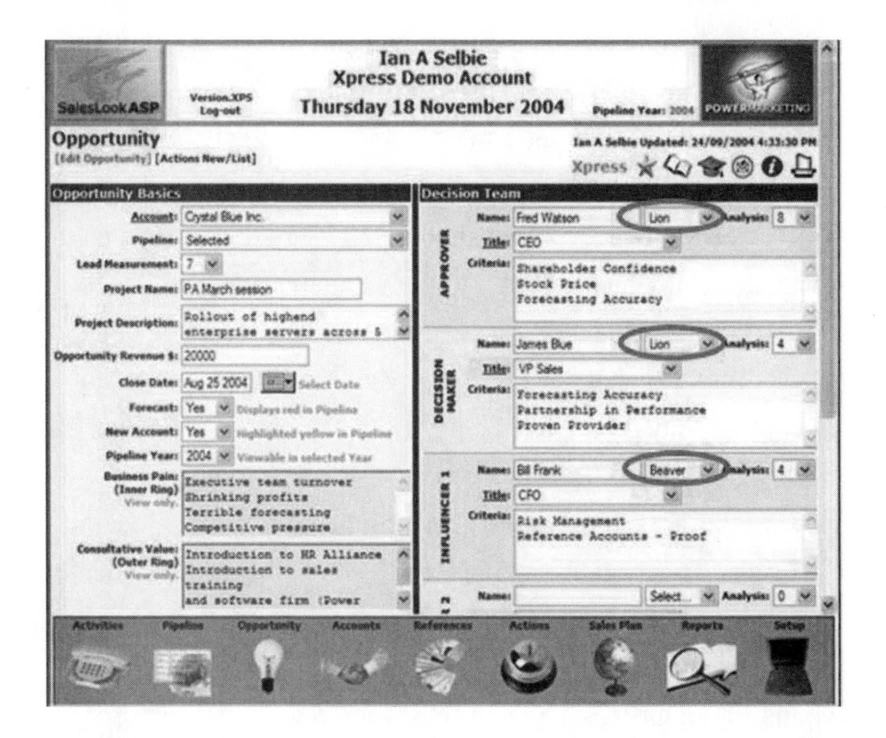

To fine-tune this exercise, there are 16 quadrants, thus you can be an otter, with a little lion in you as well. So why is any of this important for sales people? Let's reexamine the job description of a sales person.

1) Revenue
2) Relationships
3) Reporting

Relationships are an essential component of every sales person's job and so we must become experts at developing and maintaining them. If you prepare a proposal for a beaver, for example, what should it look like? Well it had better be thick, with a lot of proof, because the beaver needs to reduce risk. Industry research and written letters of reference are needed to support your proposition. The beaver will read the entire proposal, so remember, no fluff, just the facts. What about a proposal to an otter? Should it be the same as the proposal for a beaver? Not at all. If you can put your proposal on video tape and make it a fun experience it will have more impact. Use graphics and images, keep it short and be sure to incorporate their ideas into the proposal. A lion, turn your proposal upside down. Put the price on the cover letter, because they are going to go straight to that page anyway. Make sure to leave the lion in control, they do not like being put in a corner. The golden retriever needs to see team harmony in your proposal. How will your proposal help everyone get along better together? Make it feel right. This exercise applies to all people in your life. I have 4 children, 3 girls and a boy. My oldest girl is an otter, just like her mother, the second oldest girl is a lion, just like dad, my youngest daughter is a golden retriever a real sweetheart; and my son is already showing signs of being a beaver, so you can imagine my house is a regular zoo!

BUSINESS AND INDUSTRY KNOWLEDGE

Up to this point in the chapter we have been discussing relationships, communications, persistence, organization and confidence as being essential in professional sales. The consultative approach to selling infers that the sales person is acting as a consultant/advisor to his or her client. To do this, the consultative sales person requires a strong inventory of business and industry knowledge. This is one of the reasons we believe strongly in verticalization or segmentation of the sales force. Simply said, assign vertical markets to sales people so they can become very familiar with an industry, enabling them to bring this added "currency" to the table. For example, if your products

and services address the needs of several markets, assign markets directly to sales people, such as legal, medical, financial, manufacturing or technology. This will enable sales people to develop industry specific knowledge, helping them call high and bring specific value to the industry they are focused on. This alone will help differentiate the consultative sales person from other generalists calling on these same customers.
As described in the Value Proposition chapter, calling at executive levels is most effective, especially when consultative sales people are able to converse with senior management of companies with a sound understanding of business. We recommend sales people who are seriously committed to becoming consultative; enroll in executive MBA or other executive management training programs. Not only will this fine-tune your business management knowledge, it will also create an excellent opportunity for high level networking.

THE SEVEN "R's" OF THE CONSULTATIVE MODEL

In elementary school we all learned our three "R's:" reading, 'riting and 'rithmatic. Consultative selling has seven "R's":

1) Relationships based on trust, integrity, honesty and open, two-way communications with your customer at senior levels.

2) Research involves knowing your client's industry, their company, their competitors, their challenges and business pain, their budget, their decision makers, their time lines, and who you're competing with.

3) Recognize how you, your company and your products and/or services can address their business pain.

4) Recommend, through a well designed proposal that starts with your client's business objectives and challenges, how your solution will address their needs in a quantifiable manner complete with written proof from other clients.

5) Reference. Develop clients into reference accounts by managing their expectations and asking for a reference letter as a proactive part of your follow up, on a regular basis.

6) Repeat. By performing proactive account management, addressing outstanding issues and identifying new needs, you will generate repeat business with the customer.

7) Referral. Through a value-rich relationship with the client, you will earn their trust and put yourself in a position to ask for referrals into other organizations.

I mentioned one of Power Marketing's clients, Loney Financial Corporation in the value proposition chapter. Their president Dan Loney understands the seven "R's" of the consultative model. Dan does a wonderful job of account management, in fact he brings his clients business without them asking for it. This creates what I call a "loyalty vacuum." Due to the fact that Dan provides his clients with leads and new business, they in turn provide Dan with an amazing amount of referrals, not to mention their repeat business and continued loyalty. Dan has completely eliminated cold calling from his game. He spends his business development time calling on nothing but referrals from existing clients. The result, a 40 to 50% closing ratio. What's your ratio? I wish my ratio was this good.

CONSULTATIVE SALES SKILLS ASSESSMENT

1. Think about your company and score the average confidence level of your sales force.

- ❑ Needs dramatic improvement
- ❑ Needs moderate improvement
- ❑ Fine-tuning only
- ❑ No need for improvement

2. How does your sales force consistently measure the quality of leads they focus on?

____

3. When it comes to communication skills (listening, questioning and presenting) select the answer that best describes your sales force:

- ❑ Needs dramatic improvement
- ❑ Needs moderate improvement
- ❑ Fine-tuning only
- ❑ No need for improvement

4. How many current letters of reference from existing clients do you have and use as a proactive proof source to prospects?

- ❑ We've never asked for one
- ❑ We have a few, but don't use them proactively
- ❑ We have many, but don't really use them proactively
- ❑ We have many and color copy them, and use them on a daily basis.

5. Think about the opportunity pipeline which classifies deals from interested, coached, qualified, selected and closed, and think about your sales force. What is your interested to closed ratio? How many new prospects do you need to meet to end up with one closed?

- ❑ 10+ to 1 (we work very hard and too often are spending time on the wrong deals)
- ❑ 6 to 1 (we get a few referrals and also cold call to find our leads)
- ❑ 3 to 1 (we get many referrals, and so our attractive ratio)
- ❑ 1 to 1 (we are a selling machine and never lose a single prospect)

CHAPTER SIX

Sales Tools

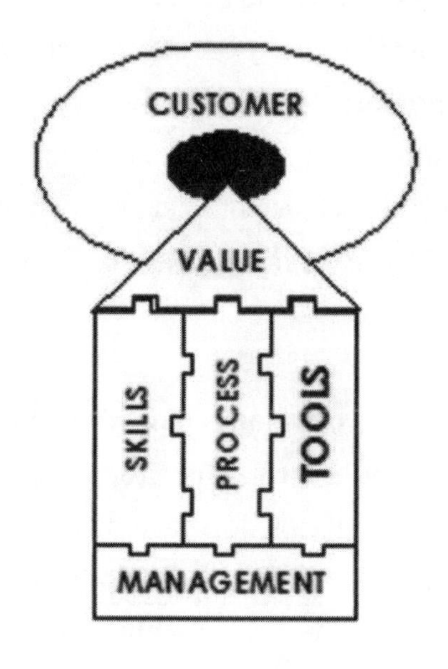

Every professional uses a set of tools. Doctors' tools range from elaborate x-ray equipment to a simple patient questionnaire; major league baseball players use bats, gloves and spikes; and lawyers use information, evidence and witnesses. What do sales people use? In our experience it ranges dramatically from their spoken word to reference letters, technology and leveraging their executives. A sales tool can be best defined as anything that can help a sales person win business, But the tool must be used with integrity. One way to consider highly effective sales tools is to put yourself in the position of buying something. What helps to convince you to select one product, company or person over another? A glossy brochure? Letters of reference? A well worded proposal? An impressive presentation? A killer web site? A clear message? A stable company? A sales person who listens and understands your needs? A great warranty? A money back guarantee? I'm sure most of these would effect how you buy.

Prior to creating any sales tools, companies must initially have a clear understanding of their value proposition. Second, the message of the value proposition must be consistent across all sales tools utilized. Beyond these two factors, companies need to consider the target person within the customer's organization that the sales tool is designed to influence. In the Value Proposition chapter we describe the difference between executives and influencers. If your sales tool is targeted at executives, then it must speak their language, address needs at their level, and be understandable to them. Good sales tools educate, inform, provoke thought and of course influence. High technology can play a multitude of roles as effective sales tools, but sales tools are not limited to technology. Highly effective sales tools can be the right 5 questions to ask an executive in order to create awareness and urgency of their business pain. They can be letters of reference as objective proof of value sources. The best thing about good questions and reference letters is that they require no technology, nor do they require a financial investment.

THE REFERENCE LETTER

We encourage our clients to diligently develop a library of reference letters. So when is it appropriate to ask for the letter? Tell your customer when they're still a prospect that your company would like to earn a written letter of reference from them upon their satisfaction of your products and/or services. This sets the stage, but also it communicates to your prospect that you don't just want to sell them something; you are setting the bar high and want to be held accountable. Once the customer is satisfied with your products and/or services ask them for the letter of reference. It should be a one page letter written by the client describing the measurable impact your solution has had on their business. We always ask for 2 originals, as we keep one in the original archive and the second we get color photocopied and distribute them to every sales person on the team, thus leveraging our proof sources. Our software, SalesLookASP stores a reference letter library providing access of every reference letter to every sales person across the company.

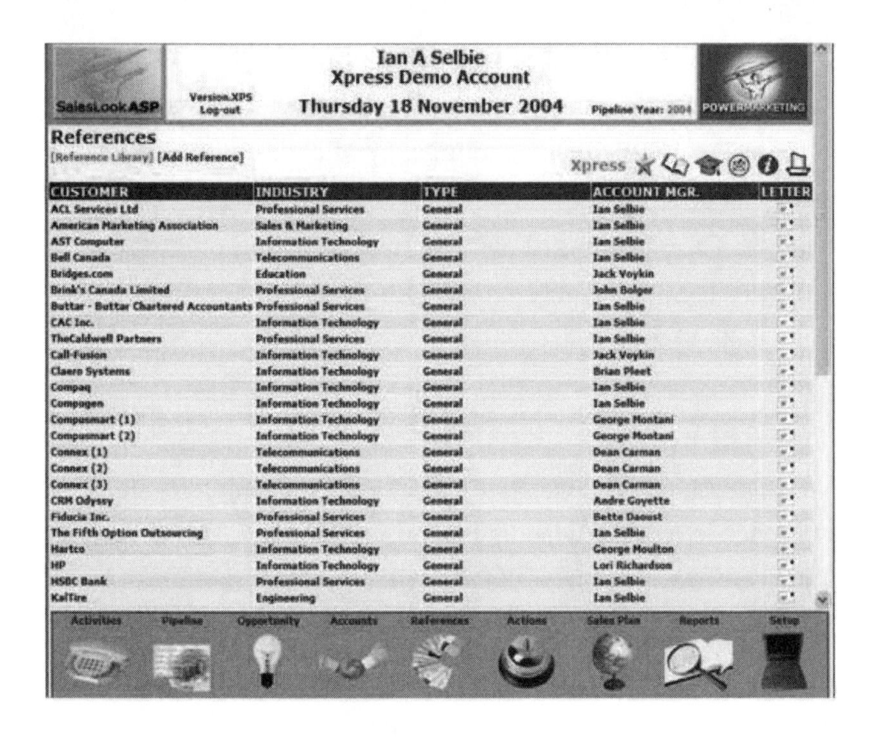

CUSTOMER	INDUSTRY	TYPE	ACCOUNT MGR.	LETTER
ACL Services Ltd	Professional Services	General	Ian Selbie	
American Marketing Association	Sales & Marketing	General	Ian Selbie	
AST Computer	Information Technology	General	Ian Selbie	
Bell Canada	Telecommunications	General	Ian Selbie	
Bridges.com	Education	General	Jack Voykin	
Brink's Canada Limited	Professional Services	General	John Bolger	
Buttar - Buttar Chartered Accountants	Professional Services	General	Ian Selbie	
CAC Inc.	Information Technology	General	Ian Selbie	
TheCaldwell Partners	Professional Services	General	Ian Selbie	
Call-Fusion	Information Technology	General	Jack Voykin	
Claero Systems	Information Technology	General	Brian Pleet	
Compaq	Information Technology	General	Ian Selbie	
Compugen	Information Technology	General	Ian Selbie	
Compusmart (1)	Information Technology	General	George Montani	
Compusmart (2)	Information Technology	General	George Montani	
Connex (1)	Telecommunications	General	Dean Carman	
Connex (2)	Telecommunications	General	Dean Carman	
Connex (3)	Telecommunications	General	Dean Carman	
CRM Odyssy	Information Technology	General	Andre Goyette	
Fiducia Inc.	Professional Services	General	Bette Daoust	
The Fifth Option Outsourcing	Professional Services	General	Ian Selbie	
Hartco	Information Technology	General	George Moulton	
HP	Information Technology	General	Lori Richardson	
HSBC Bank	Professional Services	General	Ian Selbie	
KalTire	Engineering	General	Ian Selbie	

We use these letters in a number of ways. The color library of letters goes on every sales call that our people make, showing prospective clients objective proof of our value on the first call. On qualifying opportunities, we create and present our prospective clients with a proposal. As a part of the proposal we include relevant copies of letters of reference. If you have been in a position to hire people, your have probably had the experience of reading stacks of resumes, trying to determine who to interview. I've read many resumes in my time and I must tell you that when I receive a resume from someone who has also included letters of reference, I read the letter of reference before I read their resume in more detail. It creates proof and provides a reduced sense of risk. As mentioned they can be scanned into a computer database and leveraged across the sales force.

SUCCESS STORIES

A success story is similar to a letter of reference in that you are leveraging existing customers in a way that provides a sales tool to be used with prospective customers. This proof of concept can be documented in a number of ways, ranging from compiling printed success stories, to integrating them into a catalog, sorted by industries or applications. By utilizing technology, a company can create a database of success stories and enable their sales force with access over the network. This creates a highly effective way to leverage successes across an entire sales organization. Regardless of the format, a success story needs to clearly describe how your solution has made a measurable difference to your customer's business. A success story should contain four elements:

1) A description of the customer's business, the business challenges and/or objectives your solution addressed.

2) A description of your solution; what it consisted of (advice, products, services, support, maintenance or project management.)

3) A derived outcome for the customer as a result of your solution (time & money savings, effort reduced, productivity gained) in measurable ways.

4) A stated direction from the customer as to how they plan to continue the relationship (on-going benefits expected and the role your company will continue to play)

THE EXECUTIVE WHITE PAPER

First, I'd like to start by stating what an executive white paper is not. It is not a brochure, or a "hard sell" tool. An executive white paper is a collection of wisdom on any topic. The topics are only limited by your imagination. They can focus on a specific business problem, an industry trend, a new technology or a business process. For example, the following white papers entitled; "The Seven Deadly Sins in Selling" and "Financial Convergence, are you ready for battle."

In developing a white paper, you must first decide who your target readers are. Are they executives? What kind of executives: CFO, CIO, VP Sales, VP Operations, VP Human Resources, or Company Presidents? The topic needs to address specific issues these people deal with or issues they need to prepare for. Be sure to consider the level of sophistication of the target readers. Are you aiming at technology firms, industrial equipment firms, pharmaceutical companies, governments, health care, resource based companies or retail? Extra planning will help with the wording and examples you may use in your white paper.

Once you've identified the target audience you need to focus on a specific issue, a business problem or opportunity, or an industry trend, etc.. There are four objectives to keep in mind when developing a white paper:

1) You want to educate the reader, not sell them anything
2) You want to create or reinforce a specific business "pain," challenge or opportunity
3) You want to create urgency of the business pain
4) By virtue of the fact that your company wrote the white paper, you will have positioned yourselves as the experts, and who better to call than the experts?

The white paper must have stand alone value. While reading a white paper, it should stimulate thought and provoke the readers to consider their own organization. To encourage this process, the white paper is a great place to nest a few of your "killer questions." Utilize credible proof sources, such as industry research, perhaps by using a chart or graph and even a few quotes from your existing customers, with name, title and company. Keep it brief, no longer than 10 pages, and no hard selling or throwing "cheap," "manipulative" closes or offers at the reader. You can mention how you may be able to help them and how to get a hold of you, but keep it real soft.

THE CORPORATE PRESENTATION

Why does a company need a presentation that describes who they are, what they do, how they do it and who they have served well? In the value proposition chapter of this book we described the importance of having a value proposition and knowing what it is, not simply guessing or believing your own brochures. The second step in any sales process is consistently positioning your company's value proposition. The key words here are "consistently" and "positioning." If you don't have a tool to help every sales person position the same message, how can you expect it to be consistent? The real objective of a company presentation, or as we fondly refer to as "the pitch," is to prompt the sales person in what to say. Of course the slides will have charts and models that help describe your message and enhance overall communication, but the most important element of any presentation is the presenter. Most presentations today are a collection of slides, focusing on communicating who the company is, what they do, what their products and services include, how big their revenues and profits are, what their stock performance has been, who their executive team are, and perhaps who some of their customers are. But in general they fail to address the issue of the audience's business issues. A good presentation spends a little time at the beginning introducing the company and who some of their customers are to create a sense of credibility. Then the focus should switch completely to the audience or the customer. What are the customer's issues, challenges and objectives? Doing this generates interest by sending the message that you know their world, their situation and that you have an in depth understanding of what keeps them awake at night. Now your audience is ready to listen to you, to engage in discussion, because you have created relevance with them and you're not just there to pitch your products and/or services. Once you have communicated your understanding of their situation and needs, then it's appropriate to present how you can address these needs and solve their business challenges or enable a business objective. You've earned the right, which is something far too many sales people fail to do. A good presentation is interactive; it asks the audience questions, provokes thought and generates discussion. You can also add some of your "killer questions" into your presentation. At Power Marketing we have a few slides we use after we've presented a concept or a business challenge that ask the audience questions. One of our favorites is "If your sales force were arrested for selling, would there be enough evidence to convict them?" It's in huge letters on a slide all by itself. We recommend your presentation aproximately 10 slides long. If you are presenting to a large audience, at a seminar or speaking engagement, your presentation can run on your notebook computer connected to a data projector, allowing you to present to hundreds of people. This same presentation can be printed and used for one-on-one presentations across a desk or table at a restaurant. The same tool, the same message, regardless of setting.

THE WEB SITE

The web has become the norm today, as dial tone was years ago. If you're like me, you get far more emails than phone calls. Rather than phone tag, email is a virtual conversation that eliminates the time zone issue. The company web site is commanding attention and budget to keep current, appealing and interactive. Traditional marketing budgets are spent in television, radio and print advertising, direct mail, seminars and workshops and high gloss printed brochures. A growing percentage of these funds are being spent on the company web site, or more specifically, the company's e-business strategy. We are only scratching the surface on the internet. Using the Internet to browse a prospect's site prior to meeting with them helps you to prepare for a meaningful discussion. What about your company's web site? Does it educate the visitor? Does is help qualify and motivate them? Does it provide choices for them to access information? Does your web site ask questions in a way that helps build a profile on who they are, what they do, what their needs are and where they are in their processes? A good web site should help the sales force with beginning the qualification and education processes. With e-commerce, many websites process the client's orders as well. Where does this leave the future of a sales person you ask? Interesting question. Yes it is a high tech world, but there is no doubt that selling is a high touch profession that can leverage technology to enhance the selling process. Wouldn't it be great if a sales person went into his office in the morning, or at least log on using the internet, and found 10 high quality leads that were somewhat prequalified and just waiting to be called. Would this help the sales process? As one of my kids would say, "duh dad!"

CUSTOMER RELATIONSHIP MANAGEMENT (CRM) OR SALES MANAGEMENT SOFTWARE

I'd like to draw an analogy between selling and golf. If a golfer has a slice, which means the ball curves off the fairway into the rough, or worse yet the trees, should he or she run back to the pro shop to buy a great Big Bertha? What happens to the slicer with a Big Bertha in their hands? The ball goes further into the trees, or they become more efficient at being ineffective. So if a sales team does not have an effective sales process, will a power tool like technology help them? No way! Prior to a company trying to automate the sales force, they must have their sales process well defined, documented and ensure that the process is consistent across the sales force.

After this has been accomplished, which in itself does not happen overnight, the software a company selects must incorporate or be modified to incorporate the appropriate selling methodology. If you don't have a consistent, well defined sales process and a selling methodology for the company, then you're really not ready for total sales automation or a customer information management system. Many recent surveys reveal that over 70% of CRM or sales automation initiatives fail to meet the companies' expectations due in most part to the point we just raised. Furthermore do we want sales people spending more time in front of their computer screens than in front of prospects and customers? When I look at a sales software system, I always ask myself the question, "Will this help me win, or is it just simply admin?" After all, it is sales people who are the primary users of such a system, and we do not want to turn expensive sales people into data input clerks.

There is a wide range of products offering technology solutions for sales organizations, from contact management software all the way to enterprise relationship management software (ERM) Most of these systems offer contact management functionality, calendars and scheduling functionality, and simple correspondence management which automatically send emails, faxes and letters. Some of these systems offer complex opportunity management, which is the ability to track the various prospects your sales force is working on. Some also provide useful functionality around the task of account management and customer service, marketing and support. Most of these systems require modification or tailoring to incorporate your selling methodology and sales process.

In 2000, Power Marketing launched a sales management software system, SalesLook, something our clients had been asking us to do for sometime. In 2004 we launch a dramatically improved version entitled SalesLookASP, which is a much easier to use and implement web based version. We promise to never turn sales people into data input clerks!! It's clearly about giving sales people a tool that will help them focus, plan and succeed, while providing management with the required information to predict the business and track goals and activity progress. Going back to our golf analogy, we call this finding the "sweet spot." In the late 90's and early 2000's CRM really picked up speed, but really failed to measure up despite huge budgets and project overruns. The emergence of the ASP business model was one of the true sustainable outcomes of the dot com era. This ASP model paved the way to a new, less hassle, little to no IT department support, incredibly economic approach to CRM or said more specifically, sales management system. Our design spec for SalesLookASP was simple:

- The software is for salespeople not techies
- Keep it simple to use and administratively light
- Realize the more time in front of computer, the less with customers
- Ensure it integrates to Microsoft Outlook and standard web browsers
- Make it very inexpensive (less than the price of a coffee per day)
- Embed the proven and highly effective Power Marketing methodology
- Build in automatic management rollup and forecasting capability
- Help sales people win, don't give them more admin.!!!

Well, we did all this and more. See for yourself, take a test drive today www.powermarketingworld.com.

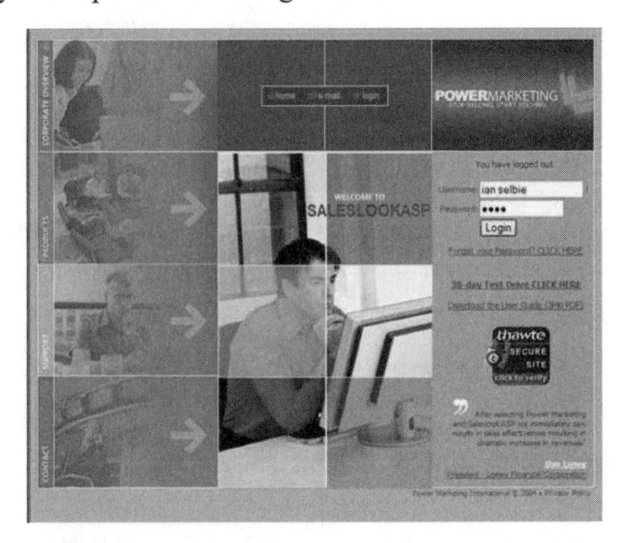

THE PROPOSAL

Think about your proposals. Are they truly a proposal? Or are they not much more that a quotation with product descriptions and related pricing? When creating proposals, do you recreate the "beast" every time? There are wonderful productivity gains to be had by using a proposal template, which is reusable. In our experience 75% to 80% of a proposal is the same for every client. Having a library of well developed and reusable templates, helps the sales people produce a high quality proposal in a timely manner.

As mentioned earlier, the sales process includes: proactive lead identification, positioning the value proposition, customer needs assessment and qualification, create and present proposal, earn customer's commitment (closure) deliver solution/ engagement, proactive account management and leveraging reference accounts. Also mentioned in this book were the seven deadly sins in selling. Sin number four is "The Premature Proposal Trap." Before sales people get overly excited about the potential of developing a proposal for someone, they need to have conducted a customer needs assessment and qualified the opportunity. Once complete, they are ready to create the proposal and arrange to present it in person to the decision making team. There are many ways to write proposals and there is merit in using a proposal template. To assist you in developing a proposal template here are the key elements that need to be included, otherwise known as the Seven P's of the proposal:

1) Purpose. In an executive summary or cover letter, overview the purpose of your proposal in the customer's terms. How will your solution impact his need?

2) Pain. Frame your understanding of the customer's business challenges & objectives.
3) Positioning. Fully describe the value that your solution offers, don't assume they know! (This is the written version of your pitch)
4) Plan. Provide a description of your proposed solution and the required time line and implementation schedule.
5) People. Highlight the account team involved from your company, include bios of the team underscoring relevant experience.
6) Pricing. Clearly state the required investment to implement your proposed solution complete with terms and ROI metrics. If return on investment information is not clear, utilize other client metrics as a model.
7) Proof. As an addendum to your proposal include relevant copies of reference letters from other satisfied customers.
Remember, a proposal is not a quotation with product numbers, specifications and pricing. It's a written document that supports your proposition for why they should select you as their solution partner. In our experience a proposal template can be 80% reusable from deal to deal and will range in size from 8 to 12 pages without reference letters. Always remember to present your proposals in person to the team making the decision. Don't trust others to do your job.

ASSESSING YOUR CURRENT SALES TOOLS

1. How effective is your current investment in sales tools?

- ❑ We don't have sales tools
- ❑ We have some sales tools, but the sales people do not see them as useful
- ❑ We do have sales tools and they are somewhat helpful
- ❑ The sales people love them; they help them achieve their revenue targets

3. How has your company incorporated proof into your current sales tools? i.e. Quotes from customers, or letters of reference.

____

3. What is the most effective sales tool your company has and why?

____

4. What key sales tool is missing? What would be a real sales weapon?

____

5. Thinking about your company's utilization of sales force automation, select the answer that best describes your return on investment.

- ❑ We have not automated the sales force, sales people use computers primarily for letter writing, email, proposals and presentations.
- ❑ We have invested in technology for contact management, but it doesn't really help us run the sales organization beyond a few tasks such as time management and contact database.
- ❑ We have invested in a sales automation system, and it has failed to meet our expectations, clearly not providing a return on investment.
- ❑ We have invested in a sales automation system, and it exceeded our expectations, thus providing a measurable return on investment of:_________% over 12 months.

CHAPTER SEVEN

Sales Management

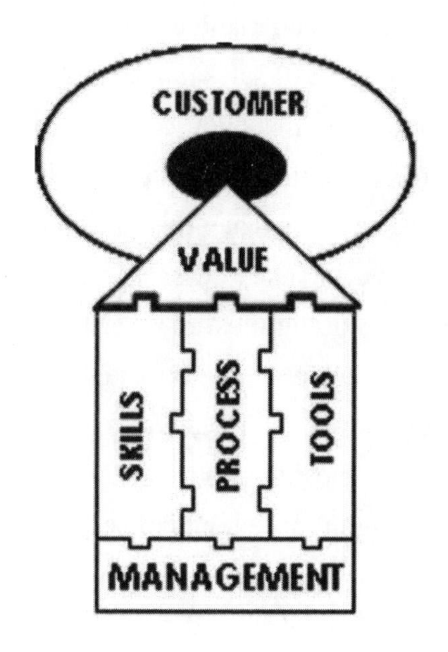

Who is the best sales manager you've ever had? Why? Who is the worst sales manager you've ever had? Why? I can speak from experience on the difference between good and bad sales management. The difference is dramatic. I have worked for a bad one and a good one in succession at the same company. It felt like two different companies. I went from wanting to leave the firm under a bad manager to growing as a professional and finding a new level of confidence, thanks to working for a good sales manager. A sales manager has a very important role to play. Being a top performer at selling does not necessarily translate into effective sales management. In fact, parenting and sales management have more in common than selling and sales management. We have seen many companies promote their best sales person into the role of sales manager. Most companies fail to provide this new sales manager with the required leadership training and coaching tools to be effective. Therefore one of two things usually happens when this investment in training and tools does not occur. The new sales manager becomes a "do it yourself" manager, doing most of the selling and eventually burning out, asking the company to make him a sales person again. He did not know how to lead a team of sales people who used to be his peers, causing him to try to make up for lack of leadership by putting in more hours of selling time personally. The second thing that can happen is the new sales manager becomes a "numbers dictator" and commonly says to his sales people "Your sales numbers are terrible this month. What are you going to sell next month?" This certainly doesn't sound like coaching to me. To add insult to injury, the company has taken the new sales manager's selling performance off the front line and if he is not properly prepared for his new role as a leader, he will probably contaminate the rest of the sales force. It can have devastating results, but many companies do it this way.

We define good sales management as a proactive coach and mentor of the sales process. In order to do this effectively, there needs to be one "best practices" sales process. Otherwise, you're asking too much of the sales manager. As we have already mentioned, most companies have as many sales processes as sales people, with every sales person doing it his own way, with no consistency across the team. Imagine each sales person playing a different sport, with one playing baseball, another basketball, another hockey and yet another is a snow boarder. How can we expect a coach to be an expert at all four? How many sales people does your company have? How many sports are being played? Does sales management stand a chance at being highly effective?

Like sales automation software, you start with a streamlined, documented sales process. Only then can a sales manager become a proactive coach and mentor.

What single element is critical in order for a sales manager to lead a sales team? In one word, "Respect." Respect is the essence of leadership and it is not given by followers. It is earned by the leader. You parents will identify with this example. If children do not respect their parents, whose fault is it? There are times I'd like to say it's the children's fault, because they refuse to listen, but when I really think about it, it is due to me thinking my children owed me respect when I had not earned it. Respect has to be continually earned by parents, who are the leaders of the family and the same is true for sales managers. We must earn the respect of our sales people on a continuous basis.

COACHING

What does coaching really mean? Growing up, most of us had coaches in the various sports we played, and their role was to develop us as players in that chosen sport. I read a quote a while back that said "Developing people does not mean just sending them to a short course or workshop once or twice a year. Coaching brings out the best in individuals, something that instructing does not even aspire to do." I strongly agree with this. Prior to launching Power Marketing in late 1994, I had spent 18 years in the information technology industry, including 10 years with Apple Computer. I have been in 7 different sales training programs, some better than others, but there was never a follow up coaching program to help me behavioralize the methodology or process. It was up to the students to try to remember pieces and hope it would be recalled when they needed it. Did I go back and open one of those training binders? Have you? The key to developing people is coaching. Training lays the foundation and levels the playing field, but coaching takes the sales person to new levels of performance. This is true of coaching anything, baseball, golf or skiing for example.

> **"Respect is not given to a leader, it's earned."**

What does it mean to be a mentor? Webster's dictionary describes it as: "a wise advisor, a trusted teacher and counselor." We all need mentors. In fact there are actually companies in the mentoring business. If you own and/or run a company you can hire mentorship services through Dan Sullivan's Strategic Coach Program. If you are looking for spiritual coaching, the Navigator organization will provide you with regular one-on-one coaching sessions. If you're like me and trying to keep your 40 something body intact, you can find a personal trainer, or physical coach. In the same way, sales people need coaches. If you're their sales manager, who is better qualified to provide them with support than you? I have had two excellent mentors in my selling life, the first, was a man named Willie Palmarini, whom I met in 1980 when I took my first sales position at Olivetti Canada. We sold electronic typewriters and word processing equipment. Willie taught me a tremendous amount about selling in our 15 year relationship. I'll always remember him telling me; "Ian, when you're building a network of dealers to represent you, never forget the little guy, after all, he has more at risk that you." Another Willie'ism: "when it comes right down to it Ian, integrity is all we have, never lose it." Willie had an endless supply of jewels that have stayed with me. Willie was not only a mentor, but also one of my best friends, who tragically died in a car accident in 1994, but even though he is gone, I know his strength and wisdom will always be with me! My other mentor is a gentleman by the name of Ian Adam. Ian and I met while we were both working for the Vancouver Stock Exchange. Ian left the VSE to join Olivetti and I followed shortly thereafter. Eventually Ian, Willie and I worked together at Apple Computer. Ian became my sales manager at Apple, in fact, we were both in the running for the position and he won. It took me a little while to "get over it," but Ian made the transition to his new role as leader so gracefully that I quickly recognized that at the time he was more ready than I to lead. Ian was a great manager. I could be hitting my head against a wall trying to crack into a new account when Ian would say to me "Let's do a brainstorming session on it buddy." We'd sit in his office and white board the account and my existing approach. Then he'd use what I've come to call "his strategic, out-of-the box thinking" to help me develop a new strategy, which usually worked. I am glad to say that Ian is still a mentor to me to this day. We remember those special few people who have mentored us. A good way to look at it is to think of sales people as the sales manager's customers. How can you help your sales people perform to the best of their abilities and grow as a professional?

MOTIVATION

What motivates sales people? Is it money? Most of the time it is not. We asked our client's sales people this question and compiled their results, with the most frequent answers starting at the top:

1) A feeling that I've actually helped my customers/job satisfaction
2) Recognition of my accomplishments/achieving my goals
3) Personal income
4) A clear sense that the company has a focused direction and identity
5) A career path I can grow into
6) Having fun/enjoying the journey

These statistics come from over 40 sales and marketing

assessments from a wide cross section of industries. Ask any sales manager what his challenges are and he'll tell you that beyond revenue forecasting accuracy, motivating the sales force is usually near the top of his list. So if sales managers are looking for a job description beyond delivering the big number to the company, they need look no farther than the list above.

COMPENSATION

There are many ways to structure a compensation program for a sales organization. We've designed many for our clients. The key to sales compensation is that it must relate directly to the overall business plan of a company, and must incorporate the critical business directions and initiatives. Depending on the industry and margin norms within, the compensation should be tied to profitability. One of our clients is Compugen Systems, Canada's third largest national systems integrator and reseller. The computer industry continues to go through dramatic margin pressure. So the President of Compugen, Harry Zarek, bases the Compugen sales compensation plan on margin. Profitability has become one of the lead measurement criteria in their opportunity pipeline. This helps focus the sales force on the right business for Compugen. Earlier in this chapter I mentioned the importance of leaders having the respect of their leader. I can tell you every employee of Compugen has enormous respect for Harry.

All true sales organizations assign quotas, or revenue targets to their sales people, which means they are measuring their results. But, do they measure the activities that lead to these results? Most do not. We can't manage what we don't measure.

Therefore if we are not measuring the activities that lead to results, we're focusing on the end, not the means. As a sales person and as a sales manager arriving at a compensation plan that works, can be a challenge. Let me describe a plan that incorporates the concept of rewarding the right activities and results for a sales team.

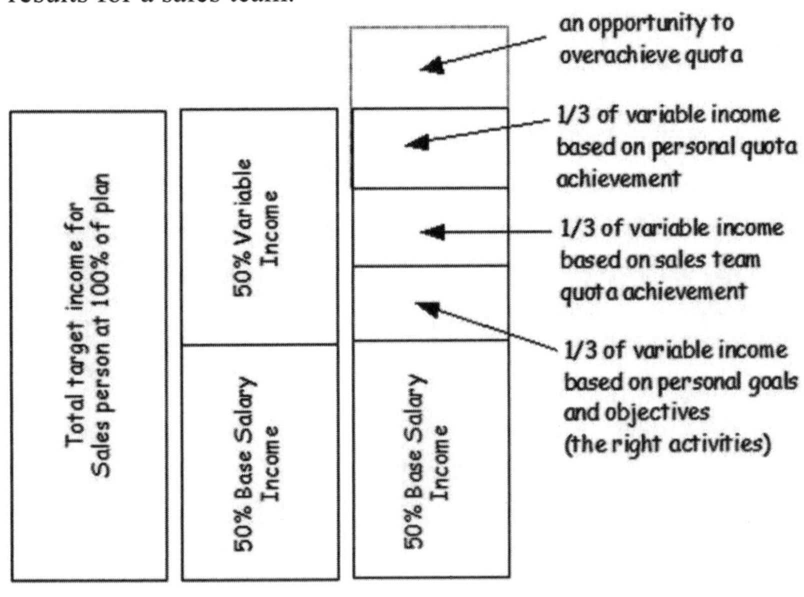

The plan I've just described provides the sales person with a personal quota and recognizes its achievement, while providing further reward for overachievement. It also helps make the sales people work as a team, perhaps teaming up on group activities, such as seminars or other group based campaigns. As well, everyone on the team co-owns the sales manager's quota. The third element is goals and objectives, which provides the sales manager with ability to fine-tune the plan for each sales person in his/her given territory and/or vertical market. This plan allows the manager to tailor it as needed. Later in this chapter we'll discuss the personal sales plan, in which one of the components is calculating how many new business meetings a sales person needs on a monthly basis to help the sales person achieve their quota. Meeting quota can be included in the goals and objectives comp plan for this salesperson and measured on a quarterly basis. Other activities such as seminars, corporate briefings, networking sessions, and speaking engagements may also be a part of the salesperson's goals and objectives. It's about determining the right activities that lead to results and rewarding the salesperson for the right activities and results.

RECOGNITION

It is amazing what the power of recognition can do. Not just those getting recognized, but for the people who want to be recognized next time. Recognition is basic to human nature. When we recognize our children for something they've done, how does the child feel? Appreciated, valued, encouraged, confident, supported? Do those five words fit into the vocabulary of a sales manager? They should! For many sales managers they do. Recognition can come in many forms, ranging from a formal "President's Club Award Ceremony," to a high five after a great sales call. Recognition is like juice to salespeople, and we all thirst for as much as we can get.

In 1990, six years into my Apple tenure, and in my capacity as a Corporate Account Manager, Apple recognized me in a way I'll never forget. It was one of those years where everything came together. My largest account grew from $300k the year before to $3.3m. In fact most of my accounts that year finished over the target we had predicted. I had an incredible team, including one of the best systems engineers Apple ever had, Andrew Bridges, who had the rare mix of a solid technical understanding, strong business knowledge and great presentation skills. One of my goals was to bring 4 corporate accounts to Cupertino (Apple's headquarters) for executive briefings, or 1 per quarter. The staff at the briefing center, who were really an extended part of the team, were Maria Murphy and Mae Grigsby. They had a great understanding for the needs of the client prior to them arriving, and getting the right Apple resources to speak to them and afterwards, managing the follow up. The other person who was instrumental in my best ever year at Apple was my sales manager Ian Adam. Without his "strategic out-of-the-box thinking" my best year would never have happened. Now back to my story. In October, 1990 the Apple Sales Conference was in Honolulu, Hawaii. In a room of over one thousand Apple Computer sales people my mug shot was displayed on the big screen and Apple recognized me as their Top Sales Person. I remember running to the front, getting up on stage and hugging, the then - Chairman and CEO John Scully. At that moment, while I was dizzy with surprise and amazement, I knew I loved selling. It was one of my proudest moments, right up there with delivering 2 of our 4 children. It felt like the Academy Awards. The rest of the conference was a dream. Clearly a great team effort and result!

Below is a picture of one of my mentors, Ian Adam and I at an Apple Reunion in 2003. Haven't we aged nicely?

Recognition is fuel for confidence and contagious as a motivator, because every sales person wants to be recognized. If your company does not have a formal "Top Guns," "President's Club" type ceremony, I'd strongly urge you to consider implementing one. It's not the award, the plaque, the trip, or the bonus that counts, but the public recognition among our peers that really makes an impact. I was doing follow up coaching for one of our clients, Compugen and was invited to attend their national sales conference. Harry Zarek, their president got up on stage and read off the names of Compugen's Top Producers, their "President's Club." It was a treat to see the faces of the winners. It was like watching eagles leave their nest, soaring higher and higher. Confidence was manufactured on the spot and motivation was spilling across the room, as the sales people who did not win that year, resolved to win the next year.

PERSONAL SALES PLAN

What keeps a sales manager awake at night? In my experience there are 4 things:

1) Achieving the large sales quota
2) Revenue forecasting accuracy
3) Motivating the sales force
4) Ensuring that the sales people have the right levels of activity... are they hunting?

After we have conducted our sales and marketing assessment, presented our recommendations to the senior management team and facilitated our two day consultative sales training program, we launch our sales management coaching program. The focus on the coaching program is QQ, Quality and Quantity. Our objective is to ensure that the salespeople have a highly effective and consistent sales process (quality) with adequate levels of appropriate prospecting activities (quantity) Activity management is the key for any company that's growing or wants to grow. Far too many salespeople are living on the laurels of past wins. They focus on their existing accounts, which if they keep buying, everything will be fine, or so they think. Do they always keep buying? And is this enough on which to base the future of the company? In the previous pages I referenced the personal sales plan. Every business writes a business plan and refines it on at least an annual basis. Divisions within the company also write their business plans, outlining their contribution to the overall company. We believe every salesperson should also have a personal "business plan."

We call it "The Personal Sales Plan." If you fail to plan, you plan to _____? This is certainly true in the world of selling. The most successful people throughout history have consistently documented their goals and remained focused on achieving them. Is a revenue target a goal? Our answer is that it's only one of them. It is in fact the end, but what about the means? Enter the personal sales plan which has five elements:

"If you fail to plan, you plan to _____."

1) New Business Revenue and Activity Quotas
2) Existing Customer Revenue and Activity Quotas
3) Personal and Team Activity Quota
4) Information Reporting Policy
5) Professional Development Plan

When you come right down to it, selling is a numbers game, and like most numbers games, there are formulas that enhance the predictability of success. Below we describe an example of a personal sales plan, along with a template to calculate one for a typical sales person within your organization. First, assign each salesperson an annual sales quota. There are many factors that influence an annual sales quota; previous year's achievement, historic growth or decline in a given sales territory, vertical market health, new products and services, competitive landscape etc.. Second, analyze the annual sales quota to determine the likely forecasted achievement from existing customers, thus calculating the new business target. Determine the average new account revenue annualized. When signing on a new account, what is the first year's revenue likely to be, or better yet, using historic data, what has it been? This will tell us how many new deals/customers we need to achieve the new business target. Next, think about the opportunity pipeline. What is each salesperson's "interested to closed" ratio. Interested is defined as a prospect willing to meet with you. Closed is defined as ink on a contract or an actual deal. How many interested prospects are needed to result in one new deal, given the fact that many will not make it all the way through? We then take the number of deals or new customers required to achieve the new business target and multiply it by the "interested to closed" ratio or the number of new, first meetings required to close one deal. This answer is the total number of meetings required annually. Divide it by 12 for 12 months, or 10, if there are a few dead months in the year, depending on what you sell, and we will see how many meetings each sales person will require to do his or her new business target. As illustrated in the sales process chapter, in the opportunity pipeline model, the monthly meeting goal should be written into the activities section of the pipeline. When the sales person books a new meeting, and writes the name of the company into "interested," they then reduce the monthly meeting goal by one, and so on until they have reached their monthly goal. This meeting goal should be set back to the total amount monthly. This will put measurement on one of the key activities for success.

Example	The Personal Sales Plan	Template
$5m	Annual Personal Sales Quota	
$3.5m	Annual Existing Account Forecast	
$1.5m	Annual New Business Gap	
$1.0m	Annual Stretch Target	
$6.0m	Total Revenue Goal	
$250k	Average Deal/Acct Size (annualized)	
10	Number of new Deals/Accts Required	
6:1	Interested to Closed Ratio	
60	Number of new Meetings Required	
6	Number of new Meetings Monthly	

Here is how the Personal Sales Plan looks using SalesLookASP:

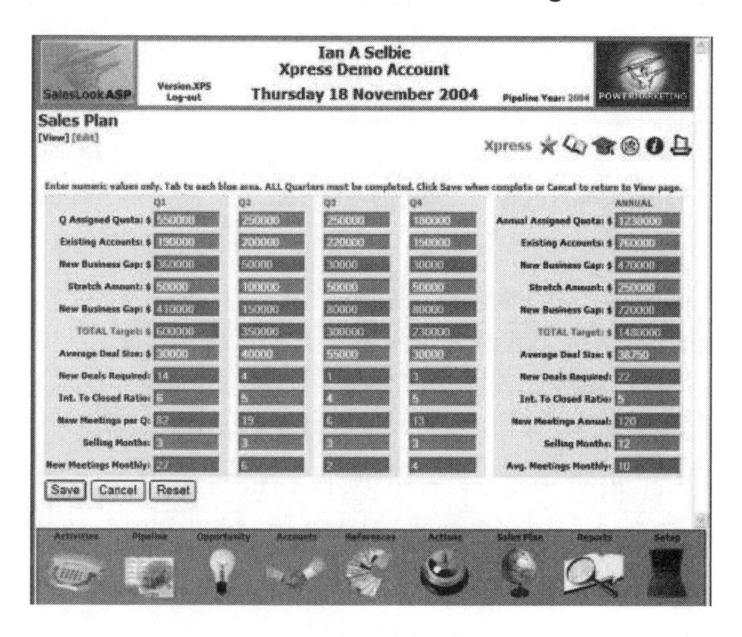

The next measurable element of the personal sales plan is account management. In our example, we noted that from the $5,000,000 annual sales quota, $3,500,000 should come from existing customers. How, you ask? Certainly not by waiting for them to call us. We need to proactively manage the accounts on a regularly scheduled basis. We now need to calculate how many customers will contribute to the total over-achievement hunting goal of the $2,500,000. In most cases there are a few customers who drive the largest portion of the number. In this example, lets say we have 4 customers that will account for $2,500,000, and the other $1,000,000 will come from 6 other customers. In our consultative sales training program we have a module entitled "Proactive Account Management" otherwise known as "hunting on the farm."

The third element of the personal sales plan is personal and team activities. These will vary depending on the type of products and services you offer. The types of companies, the contact levels within each and the different markets or industries targeted. For example executive briefings, where you are targeting senior management for a 90 minute seminar to discuss how your solutions address their business objectives and challenges, may work in one industry but not in others. Other activities such as; trade shows, direct mail & follow up, product demonstrations, test drives, open houses, and workshops may be more relevant for your company. Whatever the appropriate activity, there needs to be a measurable component that is documented into the personal sales plan for each salesperson. These activities can also be reflected in the salesperson's pipeline.

The fourth element of the personal sales plan is the information reporting policy. Revenue forecasts, or in our world the opportunity pipeline, progress reports and expense reports should be completed on a timely basis. We are not fans of the sales call reporting, or having the salesperson document and submit every call he or she makes. The pipeline removes the need for this. Also salespeople usually feel they are being monitored too closely, or micro-managed. It also suggests you don't trust your own judgment; you hired them and now you don't trust them to do their jobs. It's different if you are putting them on a PIP (performance improvement program) but again the pipeline also reduces the need to monitor every call. When it comes to the question of how often should a salesperson submit an updated opportunity pipeline, it really depends on the time and change potential. Monthly is minimum, but weekly could be too often, because there may not be enough movement or change in one week.

The fifth element of the personal sales plan is an individual professional development plan for each salesperson. A growing organization needs to ensure the people in the organization are also growing and learning on an ongoing basis. There are many ways to develop salespeople.

We have provided a list as a set of sample topics for professional development of a sales force:

- consultative sales training and coaching
- presentation skills development
- negotiation skills development
- business writing skills
- computer use skills
- speed reading skills
- business management skills
- leadership skills
- industry specific orientation and exposure

All five elements of the personal sales plan need to be documented on an annual basis and progress should be reviewed quarterly between the sales person and the sales manager. We believe a component of a salesperson's variable compensation should be a derivative of their achievement of their personal sales plan on a quarterly basis.

ASSESSING YOUR SALES MANAGEMENT EFFECTIVENESS

1. How effective is your current sales management approach?

- ❑ Needs dramatic improvement
- ❑ Needs moderate improvement
- ❑ Needs fine-tuning only
- ❑ No real need for improvement

2. How does your company ensure the right levels of proactive activities and prospecting in a positive, motivating manner?

____

3. Does your company's current sales compensation plan reward results and the right activities?

____

4. If you asked the sales force, what would they say their sales manager does for them that helps them succeed?

____

5. If you could improve three elements of your company's sales management approach, what would/should they be?

____

CHAPTER EIGHT

Summary & Conclusions

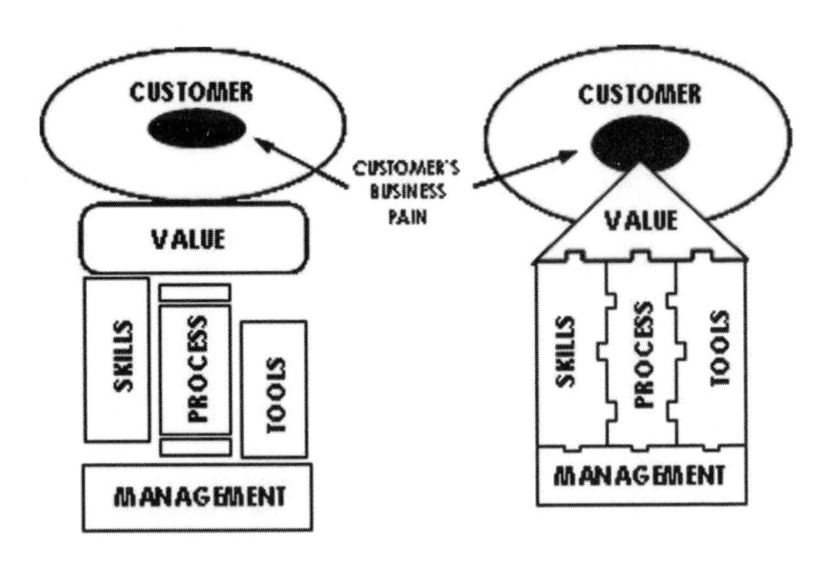

Sales effectiveness is a journey that never ends. You mean we'll never get there? Well, think about the next three points. Do the needs of your customers stand still? Does your competition, existing, new and soon to be, let you win without a battle? Does your company, its products or services change? Given the answers to these questions, is sales effectiveness a static process that once achieved is done? Never! All growing sales organizations must continually make positive strides forward in their journey and assess their progress. Remember you can't manage what you don't measure.

In examining the model of sales effectiveness for many companies from a multitude of industries, there tends to be three pieces of the model that are most suspect. The Sales Process is the area that needs improvement the most. A close second would be the sales management aspect and then the value proposition. This has varied however and in some cases the skill level was not merely a refinement task, but needed dramatic development. We have compiled a list of symptoms of an ineffective sales organization. Take a minute to reflect on them, thinking about your own organization.

TOP TEN SYMPTOMS OF AN INEFFECTIVE SALES FORCE

1) Consistently not achieving assigned sales quotas

2) Lack of confidence calling at executive levels

3) An absence of account and/or opportunity planning

4) Poor understanding of your customer's business pain

5) Poor understanding of what the customer sees as value

6) Underestimating the competition

7) Pursuing deals blindly, not selecting competitive situations carefully

8) Spending more time in the office than with customers

9) Spending more time using computer software than selling

10) Inaccurate revenue forecasting

How many of these symptoms are present in your organization? If your answer is too many, perhaps we can help. Your company may need some fine-tuning or dramatic improvement in sales effectiveness. Our sales and marketing assessment would be of great value in identifying the specific areas that need development.

CONCLUSION

We hope this book has been beneficial to you and your organization. We believe selling is a true profession incorporating integrity, trust, honesty, persistence and passion. More often than not, selling does not get the respect it so clearly deserves. If not for sales people, we'd have no customers. If no customers, we would have no company, as nothing happens without a customer.

Over 30 years ago I picked up this definition of a salesperson, which is something I am very passionate about, so in closing allow me to share it with you on the next page.

A Definition of a Salesperson

They wish their merchandise was better, their prices lower, their commission higher, their territory smaller, their competitors more ethical, their goods more promptly delivered, their boss more sympathetic, their advertising more effective, their customers more human.

But they are realists who accept the fact that none of this will ever be. Each morning they hoist onto their backs the dead weight of last year's sales record and this year's quota and go forth to do it all over again.

Yet, for all that, they are absolutely certain that tomorrow will be better and there is nothing they would rather be than a SALESPERSON!

So salespeople, keep your chin up and know in your heart of hearts that it takes a special human being to be a salesperson, and a very special human being to be a good one!

All the best, good luck and good solving!
Sincerely,

Ian Selbie
CEO & President,
Power Marketing International Inc.

Notes

Notes

Notes

Notes